DISCOVERING THE WORLD

THROUGH THE EYES OF A SOVIET DANCER

LEONID SHAGALOV

ARCHWAY
PUBLISHING

This book is a work of non-fiction. Unless otherwise noted, the author and the publisher make no explicit guarantees as to the accuracy of the information contained in this book and in some cases, names of people and places have been altered to protect their privacy.

Archway Publishing books may be ordered through booksellers or by contacting:

Archway Publishing
1663 Liberty Drive
Bloomington, IN 47403
www.archwaypublishing.com
844-669-3957

Because of the dynamic nature of the Internet, any web addresses or links contained in this book may have changed since publication and may no longer be valid. The views expressed in this work are solely those of the author and do not necessarily reflect the views of the publisher, and the publisher hereby disclaims any responsibility for them.

Any people depicted in stock imagery provided by Getty Images are models, and such images are being used for illustrative purposes only. Certain stock imagery © Getty Images.

ISBN: 978-1-6657-4626-7 (sc)
ISBN: 978-1-6657-4624-3 (hc)
ISBN: 978-1-6657-4625-0 (e)

Library of Congress Control Number: 2023911628

Print information available on the last page.

Archway Publishing rev. date: 08/29/2023

ANNOTATION

Discovering the World Through the Eyes of a Soviet Dancer is an extraordinary book by Leonid Shagalov. The book introduces the reader to the behind-the-scenes world of the ballet dancers of the famous Beryozka Dance Ensemble. The author, who worked for the ensemble for fifteen years, describes the difficult preparation for the lyrically beautiful and enchanting dance programs that have been seen by spectators in more than sixty countries around the world. The author also shares some of the many unusual situations that the ensemble's executives, artists, and crew members have experienced when traveling across different countries and continents.

The author is a dancer himself as well as a dance teacher and a participant in the events described in the book. He seeks to share his impressions of foreign travel during the early 1970s and to convey the unique atmosphere of each country, consciously or unconsciously drawing comparisons with his native country, Russia. That time Russia was a part of the USSR, The Union of Soviet Socialist Republics that led to the comparison other countries to the USSR.

Discovering the World Through the Eyes of a Soviet Dancer is based on non-fictional events and undoubtedly will provide entertainment for the inquisitive reader as well as insight into different cultures and political situations.

The book is richly illustrated with photographs by the author.

DEDICATION PAGE

As a first-time author, I appreciate the help of several important people who helped me bring this book to life.

- Edward Dayen – my friend, the publisher of the Russian newspaper "24 Hours" in San Francisco, California, who counseled me that my "stories" were detailed and interesting enough to deserve their own book

- Pavel Frenkel – my dear cousin and a published author, who helped me navigate through the publishing process

- Zinaida Fedotova – my childhood friend and a Russian Informational Agency journalist

- Natalia Zhelnorova – my friend and a noted Russian journalist
Borth, Zinaida and Natalia, published my stories in Russia online encouraging me to continue writing

- Linda (Lindochka) Davis - my English editor and a dear friend

CONTENTS

Preface xi

Part 1. Our Tour to a Flaming Continent

Chilean Diaries 1

    Landing in Chile 3

    In the Hotel 4

  The Coup, Day One 5

    The Beginning of the Coup 5

    Shots! 6

    Bombing 10

    Helicopter Attack 12

    Evening on the Day of the Coup 13

    End of the Day 13

  The Coup, Day Two 20

    After Lunch 22

    Evening 24

  The Coup, Day Three 29

  The Coup, Day Four 31

    The Murder of President Allende 33

  The Coup, Day Five 34

  The Coup, Day Six 35

The Coup, Day Seven 36

The Coup, Day Eight 39

The Coup, Day Nine 40

The Coup, Day Ten 41

The Coup, Day Eleven 42

    Departure from the Hotel 43

    Santiago Airport 44

Argentina 47

    First Rehearsal on a New Stage 49

    Presidential Elections 50

    Murder and Mourning 52

    First Performance! 53

    After the Performance 54

    Russians in Argentina 57

    Work 62

    Days Off 63

    Adios, Argentina! 65

Peru 75

    Lima 75

    Performances 76

    Thievery! 77

    The Stage is Crumbling! 78

Venezuela 83

    Rear Admiral Rudnev 83

    Separated Brothers 84

Colombia, Bolivia, and Ecuador 89

    Concerts with Security 89

    Simon Bolivar 91

    A Change of Plans 92

Costa Rica (a Surprise!)..93

San Jose, Costa Rica 94

Performances 95

The Last Performance..95

Part 2. At Home between Tours

The Flight Home 103

Where Are the Costumes? 109

Part 3. Around the World with Russian Dance

Czechoslovakia...................................... 113

Shoes!... 113

First Performance... 114

Our Travels through Czechoslovakia 115

On the "Crystal Plane" to Moscow 117

Happy to Be Home.. 118

Spain 121

Paris 129

Inside Palais des Congrès 130

Opening the Palace of Congrès: First Performance 133

Avenue des Champs-Élysées................................. 135

Zizi Jeanmaire and Roland Petit 136

Back to Champs-Élysées 139

French Music 140

A Day in the Life of an Artist 145

Popular Music on Paris Radio: Gilbert Becaud and

Jacques Brel... 147

Classics French Singers: Yves Montand, Edith Piaf,

Charles Aznavour, and Serge Gainsborough..................... 149

Youth on Parisian Radio: Mireille Mathieu, Claude
François, Gerard Lenorman, and Michel Sardou................ 155
Meeting Jacqueline Kennedy.................................... 163
Death of French President Georges Pompidou 167
An Invitation to Lunch at a Parisian Home................ 170
Demonstration, leaflet, and KGB.............................. 174
Once in the Paris Métro....................................... 179
A Theft on the Paris Métro.................................... 180
Au Revoir, Paris! 182
Returning to Moscow.. 187

Part 4. Mysterious Experiences with Victor Balashov and his Son

A New Job... 193
Performances Fraught with Injuries..................... 193
Victor Ivanovich Balashov: Healer 197
Like Father, Like Son.................................... 198

PREFACE

Coup, Murders and Mayhem: Unexpected Adventures of a Soviet Dance Company

A Russian-language newspaper in San Francisco gave me the idea to write my memoirs about my travels around the world. That is how this book began.

The Beryozka Dance Ensemble—*Beryozka* means "little birch tree"—is a troupe of dancers founded in 1948 by Russian choreographer and dancer Nadezhda Nadezhdina. The dancers are famous for their energetic and masterful dances enhanced by beautiful traditional costumes.

The Beryozka Dance Ensemble has performed in more than sixty countries. I worked with the company for fifteen years and visited only thirty-five countries, but there are more than enough memories from those experiences to share in this book! I look forward to sharing the most dramatic and the most memorable stories in the life of Beryozka.

The information in the chapter about our presence in Chile are taken from a small diary I kept while we were locked in the hotel. Unable to go outside, I took pictures directly from the window of our hotel room, from the television screen, and from the roof of the hotel, and later from the newspapers.

I kept diaries, to be honest, very rarely—only in very unusual countries like the United States or under unusual conditions like the ones we experienced in Chile during Pinochet's coup. Especially in Chile, I understood what an unusual and extreme situation we were in, but only later did I understand the danger of some of the situations, such as when, in the Santiago hotel elevator, people told me in no uncertain terms that the person with the camera would be the first to be shot, or at the airport, when soldiers searched our luggage, silently, without announcing what they were looking for.

As soon as Beryozka returned to Moscow from Chile, without taking a breath, we left for Czechoslovakia in four days. And when we returned from Czechoslovakia one month later, I realized that the severity of the political moment in Chile had passed. No one has ever discussed Pinochet's coup. Moreover, I did not have anyone in the literary world with whom I could consult. And there was never any free time. I was consumed with work—rehearsals and performances, plus caring for a ten-month-old daughter and improving our new apartment. My head was spinning!

I printed my photos, showed them to my wife, and put on the back burner for the future. And I forgot about the diary; in fact, I lost it. I found it many years later when I was collecting things for my move from San Francisco to Portland. What a coincidence in time!

Residents of the Soviet Union who did not travel abroad considered us lucky to be able to see the world. But everything was not so simple. Residents of the Soviet Union did not know the details of our tours, and sometimes our families did not know the details because we did not want to worry them.

When I worked in the tourist circle in San Francisco, I realized that my story—especially my experiences in Chile—might be important today. My job was to lead excursions around San Francisco, telling stories about city. I also drove tourists to the airport. Of course, I met tourists from South America, and from Chile too. When I told them that I was in Chile on September 11, 1973—even without naming what happened that day—I saw eyes widening in horror and two questions always followed: "Really?" and "How was it there?" In countries in South America, not only in Chile, people have never forgotten Pinochet's coup! It shook everyone, touched everyone.

I realized that I needed to describe these events. The right time has arrived.

Leonid Shagalov
Soloist dancer, teacher: Beryozka State Academic
Dance Company (1968–1982)
Portland, Oregon, USA, 2023

PART 1

Our Tour to a
Flaming Continent

CHILEAN DIARIES

*O*n September 9, 1973, we, the artists of the State Academic Choreographic ensemble Beryozka, met at Sheremetyevo-2 International Airport. We are on our way to Latin America for a tour of performances. Excitement, rushing, and predeparture fever. But Nadezhda Sergeevna Nadezhdina, the creator and Artistic Director of the ensemble, is calm, and gradually her calm is transmitted to everyone.

Even before flying to this distant continent, I knew that South America was called "A Flaming Continent," and I internally tuned in to experience the ups and downs that might occur unexpectedly. I had recently seen a Soviet documentary with this name created by famous cinematographer Roman Carmen that exposed the unrest and disorder in many countries of South America. But the disturbance and unrest that were in our path and the terrible events we would witness in the very near future, we, of course, did not know.

Four countries were planned for this tour: Argentina, Venezuela, Colombia, and Peru. The ensemble had already been to these countries; we were already familiar with the hospitality, cordiality, and warm welcoming of the Hispanics. I want to emphasize this point. Yes, there were four countries planned. But by the end of the tour, we had performed in nine countries! The governments of all the countries conducted negotiations officially (except the government of Chile, where we ended up by accident, in transit). Officials made requests to the Soviet government, and after quick negotiations with us and with our impresario, Alfonso, who, starting from Argentina, was always with us, we would be notified which country we would go to next, how many days we would be there, and how many performances we would give. Until the last week and the last country—Costa Rica—neither we nor our families in Moscow knew when we would return home.

At the end of the trip, we had already jeopardized the next trip, which was to be to Czechoslovakia. We were supposed to have five "off" days after returning from South America, and even that was a real risk. On our way to Moscow, because of the weather, we were delayed one day near Paris, which meant we had only four days left to rest and to prepare for our journey to Czechoslovakia. But that's another story. Sometimes our experiences were dramatic, and sometimes they were funny. Let's go back to our trip to South America.

So, the departure. We fly on the best Soviet aircraft—the Ilyushin Il-62 long-range jet. At that time, it was one of the largest and best in the world, the flagship of Soviet aviation. And the route was new, just mastered: Moscow to Santiago-de-Chile.

At that time, in 1973, Chile was a socialist country. In 1970, a socialist, the "First Marxist of Latin America," as he called himself, Salvador Allende, was elected president of Chile. He struck up a strong friendship with the government of Cuba and, of course, the government of the Union of Soviet Socialist Republics (USSR). Our government was extremely pleased with this unexpected "bridgehead of socialism" on a distant continent and tried its best to support the socialist system in Chile, hoping to spread its influence through this country over the entire continent. In Chile, Soviet specialists began to work in various fields: the trade navy, engineering, and even cultural development, particularly in ballet.

Our first performances should start in Buenos Aires, the capital of Argentina. But since Buenos Aires is geographically close to Santiago-de-Chile, our Ministry of Culture decided to send us through Santiago. The Russian airline Aeroflot had already established regular flights with Chile; our planes flew to Santiago-de-Chile every week. It was decided to send us that way to Argentina. The route turned out to be a little longer but less expensive. The Ministry of Culture could save money by sending us with Aeroflot and paying Soviet rubles for a longer flight and then paying dollars for the short flight from Santiago-de-Chile to Buenos Aires.

Landing in Chile

We departed Moscow late in the evening of September 9, 1973. After thirty hours of flight with intermediate landings in Rabat (Morocco) and Havana (Cuba), we finally landed in Santiago-de-Chile. It was eight o'clock in the evening. We then faced another two to three hours' of flight to Buenos Aires, where they were waiting for us and where our first performance would be held in the huge sports palace, Luna Park. But our plane was not here.

The Chilean authorities explained that our plane had not arrived; the reason was unknown. In addition, a general strike was taking place in the country. Even if our plane was at the airport, no one was there to load it; the airport movers were also on strike. We, unfamiliar with the concept of strikes, had to simply accept these travel conditions. The Chilean authorities assured us that they would send us to Argentina as soon as the strike ended. In the meantime, it was suggested that we leave all our luggage at the airport, take only our most necessary belongings, and spend the night in a hotel in the city downtown. "In the morning, when your plane arrives, you will fly to Argentina" - the Chilean authorities told us. Since we were not offered another option, we had to agree to this one.

We pulled our luggage into a room given us by the administration of the airport, and we checked out the locking system that would guard our possessions, including all the costumes for our stage performances. At nine o'clock in the evening, buses arrived in the terminal. We boarded and were driven to the city.

In the Hotel

The buses were very simple; they were commonly used for schoolchildren. But we understood that this is an unexpected situation, and during a general strike in the country, we can't count on the more luxurious touring busses we were used to.

OK, we're going. After traveling for about twenty minutes along the dark highway, we approach the city. First impression - the streets are poorly lit, and the city seems gray, nondescript. This was not the way it is in Moscow where, at the entrance to the city, eight- and nine-story brightly-lit residential buildings greet visitors. Here the houses are three- and four-story simple buildings. There is a lot of garbage on the streets; we assume it's caused by the general strike.

Nearer to the city center we pass wide, straight avenues. But most of them are not lit, and much of the pavement is torn up. Repairs? Constructions? It's all incomprehensible to us. Even here, everything is dirty. Garbage, paper, and newspapers are strewn in the streets. Only a few of the shop windows are lit.

There is car traffic, but there are a lot of people at bus stops. Their attitudes made it clear that they had been waiting for a long time. Trucks full of people driving along the streets. One truck stopped. People ran up and swore. They jump onto the trunk of the truck while it continues to moving. The truck accelerates and leaves immediately. This all gives us a sad impression of the capital of Chile.

Ten o'clock in the evening, we arrive at the hotel. Oddly enough, the hotel turned out to be very decent—an eight-story building with a marble hall, albeit dimly lit. Staff members explained to us that, since we arrived late, the restaurant is already closed, and we can't get dinner. "Please take a glass of water, dear famous performers." So, instead of dinner, we received a full glass of cold water and an order-invitation to appear in the morning for breakfast. And so, we went to our rooms.

We found the hotel to be clean, quiet, and calm. It seemed they were trying not to disturb the rich guests. They were fencing themselves off from the life that was boiling in the city.

The Coup, Day One

The Beginning of the Coup

We awoke at nine on the morning of September 11 expecting information about our departing flight at the airport, but there is still no information, which means that our plane is not at the airport. We are restricted to the hotel and not allowed to go outside. From the windows we watch the local life. All seems normal and calm. A lot of well-dressed people walking on streets.

Shots!

At 9:30 in the morning, suddenly, shots rang out. Single shot and short machine gun bursts. And it's close! Shots seem to come from a nearby street, right around the corner. Our hotel is two to three hundred meters from the presidential palace La Moneda. We cannot see from our window who is shooting, but we can clearly see soldiers on the corner hastily setting up a machine gun. People are fleeing, mainly from the center of the city and from the presidential palace. Some run with their hands up. But we see little fear in their actions; it is as if they act out of habit. We see that shops and kiosks are closing and people are still running. But cheerful music continues on television, so we conclude that everything is in order. Only one television channel is working, and it is broadcasting cartoons! Although we all liked the animated story of the wolf chasing a small animal (it reminded us of our Russian cartoon, "Hey, Just Wait!"), we were not interested to watch it while there was shooting in the streets. Such a strange combination—cartoons and real-life shooting! Or the cartoons are being broadcast with a special goal—to hide the events in the capital from the rest of the country? Questions—a million. Trying not to take our eyes from the television and waiting for actual news, we put our small things in bags and preparing to depart from the hotel. We hope our luggage is still safe at the airport.

One member of our group is running from room to room announcing an all-dancers' meeting in the hotel lobby. Okay, nothing new; in fact, it had been planned the day before.

But unexpected events started happening immediately. As we entered the hotel lobby, we saw the representative of Aeroflot, Vladimir Ivanovich. He had come to reassure us and explain the situation. He told us that, in Chile, at that very moment, an attempt at a coup was underway. This coup attempt was led by the Chilean minister of defense, General Pinochet. The current situation is such that Santiago Airport is closed. All flights are canceled, and we cannot fly out. Also, we cannot leave the hotel. First, it is not safe. Second, we have only transit visas, so we have no right to legally be on the streets of the city. The Soviet Embassy is blockaded—no exit, no entrance allowed. At the Cuban Embassy, a real battle is taking place. The Chilean army alleged that Cuba had been involved in interference with internal Chilean affairs and in the building of socialism in Chile. And it looked like the truth. Everybody in Chile knew that President Allende was protected by Cuban bodyguards sent by Fidel Castro. At this moment, a curfew had been established for the city of Santiago.

The only Soviet person who could move freely around the city was Vladimir Ivanovich. He was a tall, thin young man who took wide steps as he freely walked along the empty streets of Santiago. When he came to our hotel, we paid him our highest respect. For us, Vladimir Ivanovich was our only hope for leaving Chile, the only thread that connected us with our homeland. The company management told us that Aeroflot would take care of us during our stay in Chile, especially our food. After all, we had just flown out of Moscow, had not given a single performance, and had no money. But Aeroflot's resources are not unlimited. Moreover, no one knows how long we would be confined in the hotel as the political actions unfolds before our eyes. We were told there would be food, but it would be minimal. "Please do not grumble or be offended," we were told.

After this warning, we were invited to the second floor to the restaurant of the hotel. We were given half of the restaurant so that we could sit in one group. There were ninety of us: executives, dancers, orchestra members, and technical specialists. We each received one fried egg, a small bun, and a small cup of coffee. (Here's the answer to the question how do ballet dancers stay so thin!) This modest breakfast became the standard during all the days we lived in the hotel.

Breakfast went by quickly. Firstly, there was nothing to eat. Secondly, everyone was eager to find out what was happening in the city. We were eager to get to our rooms to see if there was news on the television or radio. Before we left the restaurant, we were ordered to stay in our rooms, wait for lunch, and hope that lunch would be better than breakfast.

I went up to our room, which was on the seventh floor of the eight-story hotel. The television is still working, but it still only broadcasting cartoons. Is that really so important and so interesting when the shooting continues outside our windows in the city?

I suddenly remembered my camera. I always carried it with me! *I have to shoot this "local mess,"* I thought. *It will be interesting to tell the story and show my pictures when we return to Moscow.* I grabbed my camera and ran to the elevator.

There were a lot of people in the elevator; they were all hotel workers. Seeing my camera in my hands, one of the workers said in a boring voice that the soldiers shoot first at the person with a camera. I understood. I had learned much of the Spanish language from the previous performing tour in Spain in 1971. Nervously, I tried to squeeze my camera into the pocket of my trousers. It was not easy; in those days, good cameras were quite a bit larger than the cameras of today.

At the hotel doors, our company management were stopping anyone who was trying to exit the hotel. I returned to my room and waited for news on the television. But all I saw were the same cartoons, a joyful music, a song festival from Rome, Italy. Such joyful music! This was a wild contrast! The shooting on the streets was escalating and becoming more intense, but it was not constant. There were periods of relative quiet. There was nothing to do but watch endless American cartoons.

At 10:30 that morning, finally, the cartoon broke off mid chase. The Chilean Defense Minister General Pinochet appeared on the screen—a stern face with sharp facial features. He spoke in short phrases in an intolerant voice. He, and after him, two of the army generals and the fleet admiral, announced orders that would be in place throughout the country.

The coup was spoken of as an event that had already happened, but the fighting on the streets continued, which meant that President Allende had not given up. He and his entourage were sitting in the palace and were not going to give up. In fact, during these hours, the fight for power with the legitimate Allende government had just begun. The junta was ahead of the events by announcing its victory in advance. He did this, apparently, to prevent the supporters of Salvador Allende from taking action. But this did not help the junta; in the working districts and cities, the fight continued for several more days. But we only found that out later. In the meantime, an order was issued for us, the members of the ensemble: do not even try to go out into the city. Hide all the photo and movie equipment. Do not leave the rooms. Wait for further instructions, since it was not known how events would unfold.

It turned out that the junta had presented Allende with an ultimatum. First the deadline was eleven o'clock in the morning, but then that was extended to noon. If the ultimatum was not met, they would start bombing. But our information was unclear. Would they bomb the presidential palace? What would happen to us? We were only two to three hundred yards away from the palace La Moneda! All we could do was sit and wait in complete obscurity.

Shortly before noon, I slipped out of my room with my camera in my pocket. The corridors of the hotel were empty; I believed all the guests were sitting in their rooms. So, where to go? We were not allowed in the street. The roof? I dared to hope, and—oh, miracle—the door to the roof was not locked! Several people were already standing on the flat roof of the hotel; they were obviously hotel workers. They talked among themselves. I could tell they were worried; they did not pay attention to me. They were so passionate about what was happening that they did not utter even the usual "Buenos días" ("Good morning"), a mandatory greeting from the hotel staff for guests. But I was not important to them at that time. I stayed at a distance from them so I would not interrupt them as they expressed their emotions. This was their country, and something incomprehensible was happening all around them.

After a few minutes, all the hotel workers left, and I was alone on the roof. The roof of the hotel was a like a ninth floor. The city was visible far away. I was waiting for whatever was to come next.

Bombing

At noon, so far, everything had been quiet and calm.

Two minutes after noon - a rumble in the sky! Two supersonic jets appeared! One after the other, on a low-level flight, almost touching the roofs of the city buildings, I see they head toward the presidential palace. They dropped further still. Now they are so low above the hotel that I can see the faces of the pilots. They drop bombs on the palace and fly off. Would they come back for a second round? Yes, the next round dropped more bombs on the palace. I must admit, I did not feel that any of us was safe. After all, we are so close to the presidential palace La Moneda. During the following rounds, the planes shot cannons at the palace. All in all, six or seven rounds were made. We learned later, in newspaper articles, that seventeen bombs were dropped.

Hotel employees—maids and waiters—gathered at the glass door leading to the roof of the hotel. Commenting on what was happening, they shook their heads. Their faces were full of grief.

In a moment of calm, I pull my camera out of my pocket and take some pictures of the burning city. Sadly, we could help only with sympathy.

After the bombing, as soon as the planes flew away, fierce ground shooting began again. The presidential palace is on fire. On the streets there was nobody.

At one o'clock, we are all sitting in the hotel restaurant on the second floor taking lunch. On the other half of the restaurant, across from us, sit regular visitors to the restaurant. These people are well dressed, and many sit with transistor radios pressed to their ears. The noise of battle and the hasty voice of the announcer, apparently from the scene, spread around the hall. We hear the message that the government of Allende had been given the last five minutes. The last five minutes! Suddenly, in the other half of the restaurant at a few tables, people applauded. *God*, I thought, *what kind of environment are we sitting in?* Only then, with reason, and not with our hearts, we understood: this was the richest hotel in the city, and in this expensive restaurant, of course, were those for whom the government of the People's Unity was like a bone in the throat.

Helicopter Attack

Our lunch was meagre: a small cup of soup (more like a cup of coffee), a small meat patty, a small serving (one spoon) of mashed potatoes, and a small glass of juice. After we ate, we were to go to our rooms. I, however, take up my observation post on the roof. And I got there just at the right time. At two o'clock, two large military helicopters appeared. The helicopter attack on the presidential palace began immediately and lasted for more than an hour. The helicopters flew in circles at high speed. There are no doors in the helicopters. Large-caliber machine guns are mounted in the open doorways. A soldier sits behind each one with his legs hanging out of the helicopter. The scene resembled an American movie about the Vietnam War. Only this time it's not a movie; it's life! The helicopters drop down sharply above the palace. They dive right down and veer onto their sides so the soldiers could fire into the palace from their open doorways. The noise rose in a complicated roar consisting of helicopter engines and gunfire. However, I can hear machine-gun bursts coming from the palace. It means they had not given up! They are still alive!

Next, I hear artillery shots. The smoke from the presidential palace is increasing. Another house next to the hotel lit up. Then, at three o'clock, the helicopters flew away. We could take a fresh breath, even though the shooting continued.

After four o'clock, the shooting gradually subsides. We can see a few soldiers ducking and running along the roofs of some houses. National flags appeared on some buildings. Apparently, the people in this area support the junta. In other areas of the city, no movement is visible. The general population are obviously not involved in this coup.

Evening on the Day of the Coup

September in South America is still winter. It gets dark early. I leave my unique observation post on the roof of the hotel and return to my room. I keep my television on all the time; it is the only source of information. Announcements are broadcast one after another, almost continuously. During these announcements, I can still hear single shots on the street, so I know that some people continue to fight with the junta. One of the announcements warned that electricity and gas might be cut off. Another announcement informed, casually, in passing, that there had also been an attack on the personal residence of President Allende. But nothing is known about the fate of President Allende and his entourage.

After six o'clock, when it is completely dark, the skirmish came to naught. I hear only rare single shots. No one is on the streets— no soldiers, no residents, no cars. The junta announced a curfew that would begin at 6:00 p.m. and would be in effect for... an indefinite time.

The agitation in the hotel abates. This day, full of excitement and unexpected events, is coming to an end. It had been the first military experience in the hitherto peaceful life of the Soviet dance ensemble Beryozka.

End of the Day

September 11, around 10:00 p.m. Chile's anthem is broadcast on television. We knew there would be an important message! We gather around to catch every word, every detail.

Four people—three generals and one admiral—appear sitting at a table, faces strict as they face the camera. Each of them read from a preprepared speech. Apparently, every word is very important, and they are determined to avoid mistakes. First to read was the head of the junta, General Pinochet. Here, in my words, is a summary of his speech:

> First, the junta maintains previous diplomatic relations with all countries except Cuba, which, according to the junta, helped Salvador Allende and, moreover, directed him in how to lead the country, and secretly supplied him with weapons.
>
> Secondly, in Chile, the "Congrès-president alliance" had always been indisputable. But over the past three years of Allende's authority, this order had been violated (quote) by the "Marxist follower Allende," as a result of which economics, society, and morality were destroyed. "Allende shook the unity of the nation." Therefore, the junta will fight Marxism, as Air Force General Gustavo Lee put it, "by all possible means." The junta will reconstruct the country (read, the former capitalist relations), reconstruct the "normal course of life."

After the members of the junta had read their speeches, they took an oath.

Immediately after the performance of the "new government," pictures of the weapons depot found in the personal residence of President Allende were shown. A soldier-journalist showed close-ups of all the weapons collected in one room—machine guns, grenades, bazookas (hand-held anti-tank guns), walkie-talkies. The soldier-journalist especially noted that the weapons were almost completely "*fabrication rusa*" (of Russian production).

After that, the television station showed several more cartoons. Finally, the emblem of the television station appeared on the screen; broadcast was over for the day. So ended the first day of our stay in Chile, which was also the first day of the government coup in Chile. It had been a day filled with unexpected, horrible, and bitter events.

Transit landing in Havana, Cuba. 09.10.1973

Employees leave La Moneda Palace before the attack. 09.11.1973, 10 AM

Bombing attack on La Moneda Palace. AP-09.11.1973, 12 noon

Burning Santiago-de-Chile. 09.11.1973, 3 PM

Head of the junta General Augusto Pinochet. 09.11.73, 10 PM

Member of the junta General Gustavo Leigh. 09.11.1973, 10 PM

Member of the junta Admiral Jose Toribio Merino. 09.11.1973, 10 PM

TV station logo. Santiago, 09.11.1973

The Coup, Day Two

The next morning, September 12, the city seemed extinct. We could see neither people nor vehicles in the street. The junta had announced an around-the-clock curfew; for twenty-four hours, no one had the right to be on the streets. We look out the window in a futile attempt to learn something new. At the nearest intersection, soldiers were stationed at the machine gun installed the day before; their demeanor was serious. And right in front of our window, on the flat roof of a neighboring house, another soldier walked as he kept watch.

Far away, in the square, we can see a man walking, and then another one. There is not much going on. We rush to the window at the sound of every vehicle. A Jeep passed by carrying soldiers looking up warily as they hold their rifles pointed at the sky. We hear rare single shots, and even less often, quick volleys.

But from these rare sounds, we understand that the fight with the junta—or the struggle of the junta with the people—continues, although secretly. A small plane flies overhead several times, then a helicopter. Apparently, patrols are monitoring the city.

Looking out into the street, we notice the strange behavior of the sun. It moves not from left to right, as we were used to in Moscow, but from right to left! And at noon the sun is not in the south; on the contrary, it is in the north! Of course, we knew from our lessons at school, and we ourselves had experienced during our previous tours in Australia and New Zealand three years previously, that, in the southern hemisphere, the seasons are opposite to the seasons in the northern hemisphere. When we are experiencing autumn in Moscow, people in Australia, New Zealand, and South America are experiencing spring. Having left Moscow in early autumn, we arrived in Chile in early spring. But the fact that the sun could seem to move in the opposite direction from what we were used to in the northern hemisphere, had somehow not occurred to us, and we were a little dumbfounded.

There was not even a trace of precipitation. The weather was not hot, but it was steadily warm at 15-20 degrees Celsius (59 to 68 degrees Fahrenheit). Moreover, the weather did not change much either during the day or day by day. Therefore, neither on this day nor in the following days, did the weather distract us from tracking the rapidly developing events.

The people who are staying in the hotel seem like passengers in a ship caught in a storm. They quickly get to know each other, and although they are not friends—the composition was too varied—they try to exchange information they had learned firsthand or had heard from somebody else. We hear various rumors and make various assumptions. There were street battles in the city, and workers carried weapons to uphold the legitimate authority of the government of People's Unity. Cuban extremists have settled down somewhere and are not giving up. People estimate their number 150 to 250 fighters. But no one knows for sure. The fate of Salvador Allende and his entourage is also not known. In such obscurity, half a day passes.

On television, on a blank screen, a long list of first and last names is broadcast every half hour. I counted fifty-six names. The surnames are mostly Spanish, but there are other names: English, a few Germans, and one Polish. We found out by making inquiries that these people had crossed the border illegally into Chile when the socialist president Allende was in power. "What for?" I asked one of the locals. "What do you mean, what for?" he responded in surprise. "To build socialism!"

And nobody was surprised or worried that these people had entered the country illegally. And no one was surprised that these people had left their countries, their families, maybe their jobs, and traveled to Chile. After all, it was so important to build socialism. This is how strong the dream of something that is non-existent and unrealizable can be.

However, I remembered that the same phenomenon happened in the USSR in the thirties. People came from far away. I even know cases of people coming from the United States! The difference was that everyone came to the USSR legally. Still, this adventure did not end well for everyone. Some were arrested and jailed as spies. But there were also those who lived and worked their term in the USSR and left safely for home when it was over. And there were those who left behind their children born in the USSR. The children grew up and left the USSR for the United States, proving that they were the children of American citizens. But that's another story.

After Lunch

After our meagre lunch, we watch a video on television that shows the events of the previous day. We watch the attack on the presidential palace La Moneda, although there is still no exact information that the palace had been captured by the junta troops. We see tanks on the narrow streets of Santiago along with people searching, shooting, and running around. Everybody is running in different directions, both civilians and soldiers. Residents are running from the palace, but soldiers--to the palace. A reporter who is filming is running in a line of soldiers. The camera sways with the rhythm of their running; we watch as if we ourselves are attacking along with the soldiers. A long burst of gunfire from the palace. As the reporter falls with his camera, we also "fall" to the ground. We see everything that is happening as if we are lying on our sides. After some time, the attack continues. Or maybe this reporter was killed during the attack? Time slowly passes, but the reporter does not get up. After one minute, which seemed to last too long, the view from this reporter switches to the view of another operator, and coverage of the attack continued. The shooting escalates. Then silence, relatively.

The television report then showed the personal residence of President Allende after the attack and the bombing. Some parts were damaged, but much remained. A soldier comments on the contents of the home. He counts wine bottles and coffee cans and other extravagances. Then he counts the president's (or ex-president as he calls him) suits and shirts. Still, nothing is known of the fate of President Allende! The soldier rummaging through the president's underwear. He especially dwells on gifts from Cuba, from Fidel Castro. One such gift was a personal weapon—a submachine gun with the inscription "To a friend and ally in fight from Fidel Castro." This weapon is shown close to the camera.

At four o'clock, we notice the shooting near the hotel gradually diminishes. We see some soldiers crouching and running on the flat roofs of some nearby buildings. On some other buildings, national flags are being flown. In this district, as I mentioned, people support the junta. In other areas of the city, there is no movement. The Chilean people obviously do not participate in this coup.

At around 4:30 p.m., soldiers appear on our street right in front of the hotel. We watch them from the window to see what would happen next. Slowly, with their backs to the buildings and facing the street, they move side-by-side past the hotel, lifting their carbines up to our windows. They wave their hands, ordering us to close the windows and pull the curtains. Their faces are angry and fierce. Soldiers are moving slowly, constantly looking around as they head toward a large, six-story building obliquely across from the hotel. A poster hangs on the building facade: "No to civil war! No to fascism!" We follow the actions of the soldiers with curiosity, moving from window to window, running from room to room of the hotel. Our curiosity is understandable; never before, in our own country or when we were abroad, had we been firsthand witnesses to such hostilities. We had never witnessed a coup with our own eyes.

Evening

The soldiers set up a small bazooka-type artillery and aimed it at front gate of the building that displayed the poster. Volley! The gate remains standing. Another volley! There is a hole in the gate. At the same time, the soldier who had fired the weapon crumpled and fell to the pavement. They carry him away. The remaining soldiers carefully crawl through the hole in the gate to the courtyard. A few minutes later, two men are dragged out of the building, put facing the wall, and searched. Then they are taken away. A third man was brought out. The same thing happens—they made him face the wall while searching him. Then they take him away. The soldiers enter the building. They start searching the entire building from top to bottom. Apparently, this is some kind of committee. A few minutes later, they climb out onto the roof. On the flat roof, as elsewhere in Latin America, there is a small utility building. The soldiers are trying to open the door, but it wouldn't budge. They shot at the door, but it wouldn't open. They knock out the glass with the butt of a rifle and finally get inside. A few minutes later, they crawl back out, apparently not having found anyone or anything of interest. After throwing papers and work helmets out into the street, they carefully leave the building and, just as carefully as they came, begin to go back, their backs again against the windows of our hotel.

Without warning, however, one of the soldiers, apparently reveling in a sense of power (no other explanation can be found), shot at the windows of our hotel. He fires into the room next to ours where our young girls-dancers are staying. These girls went on their first trip abroad. Everyone on that entire floor fled their rooms and gathered in the corridor. Our girls also ran out of the room, had tears in their eyes, but were trying to keep cheerful. They were sprinkled with plaster; the bullet had broken through the glass and the curtains and had knocked chunks off plaster from the ceiling. Everyone who run out into the corridor is now afraid to go back to the room.

The hotel administration ordered us to turn off the lights in the rooms and not turn them on again. We were ordered to turn off the televisions even though, on those old models, it was possible to change the brightness of the screen. We lived in this darkness for the rest of our time at this hotel.

The coup, day 2, Santiago, Curfew. 09.12.1973

The coup, day 2, Santiago. Chronicle Video on TV

The coup, day 2, Santiago. Chronicle Video on TV

The coup, day 2, Santiago. Chronicle Video
on TV, Attack on La Moneda Palace

Destroyed entrance after the attack on La Moneda

The Coup, Day Three

Thursday, September 13. Per orders, the windows, and curtains in all the hotel rooms are closed all day. We live in a state of siege. We cannot leave the building, and we cannot even look out into the street. The only "entertainment" is trooping into the room that had been shot at to look at a hole in the glass. We take pictures and discuss the frightening event.

The documentary footage of the previous two days is again shown on television. We again watch battles and the bombing of the presidential palace, tanks on the streets and right up to the walls of the palace. People are running, some leading and supporting the wounded. We see the evacuation of the Cuban embassy. There has been fighting at the Cuban embassy; there are wounded. Cubans fly out of the country on the plane we had flown in on.

The video shows patrols searching cars in the streets and searching people. Reporters announced that our Soviet Embassy is surrounded. Soldiers would not let anyone out into the street. At such moments, it is especially nice to see Vladimir Ivanovich, the representative of Aeroflot, visits us at the hotel and supports us. Since he does not live in the embassy, he allowed to walk along the street even during curfews. We once saw him walking in big steps (he is tall) along an empty street.

We were surprised to learn that the curfew had been lifted from noon to 6:00 p.m. People are allowed to go out "in case of urgent need." This peaceful announcement is made by the television "announcer," an officer in military uniform completed with helmet. He reads this announcement as if it is a military order. It seems that now, at this moment, he is immediately ready to start shooting right in the studio. A man in civilian clothes is standing next to him and commenting in a normal conversational tone on the officer in a helmet.

We did not go out, but we resumed our observances from the windows. Passers-by are rare. Sometimes cars pass by. Even less often do we see buses. We rush to the window at every sound of an engine, whether car or bus. Anything we can see helps us understand the situation.

Someone brought newspapers into the hotel. The hotel gives them out to guests free of charge. On many pages, there are pictures and stories of the storming of the presidential palace, they show tanks close to the walls of the palace, and a fire in the palace. A few pages later, in the middle of the newspaper, there are photographs and biographies of members of the junta. And on the very last page of the newspaper, positioned as something insignificant, there is a snapshot of some soldiers holding something large wrapped in a blanket. Allegedly, this is the body of President Allende, who had committed suicide. And they want us to believe it? No, that was not the President Allende's character! He would fight to the last bullet. He would defend the legitimate power of the people to the last possible opportunity. In the end, he could invite fire on himself, but to commit suicide? No, never!

In addition, reporters like to show everything openly. If Allende had committed suicide, they would have shown the body with traces of self-inflicted death. But this is not the case, so we do not believe the suicide story. Rather, we believe that Allende, the legitimate president of Chile, had been murdered.

Since the curfew in Santiago went into effect again at 6:00 p.m., in the evening, the streets were empty again, and the patrols appeared. In different parts of the city, some shots were heard. In the evening, while it is dark, with the hotel lights turned off, we watch television. The videos of the battle and attack on the presidential palace play alternately with cartoons—an unusual combination! The third day of the coup comes to an end.

At the same time, in Buenos Aires, Argentina, the sport palace Luna Park where we were supposed to be performing is empty and locked. There are no competitions, no shows. They are waiting for Beryozka.

The Coup, Day Four

Friday, September 14, brought with it a surprise. Reading of the morning newspaper was interrupted by a noise. Someone was running along the corridor shouting, "Shagalov! Shagalov!" He was looking for me! I ran out into the corridor. "What's the matter?" I asked as the man came to a halt. "A friend is waiting for you in the hotel lobby," he said, and then ran on. *Who can be looking for me? -* I wondered. *I don't know anyone in Chile.* But out of politeness I had to find out. I got into the elevator and rode down to the first floor.

And what a surprise! There was my fellow student in the Choreography Academy at the Bolshoi Theater in Moscow Sasha Prokofiev, who later became known as San Sanych Prokofiev, a famous teacher of classical dance. The children of the most famous people of the Soviet Union considered it a privilege and honor to learn from him. Sasha and I had studied in different classes, but we had spent time together for many years at school and had finished school the same year. We knew each other very well. What a joyful and rare surprise it was to meet in a distant country, and especially under such mad political conditions.

It turned out that Sasha had been sent by the USSR Ministry of Culture to Chile to raise the level of the ballet troupe of the Chilean opera theater. He had been working in Chile for several months. The coup, of course, interrupted this work, as they say, in short order. It identically interrupted work of Soviet, Bulgarian, and other specialists who provided international assistance to Chile. Together with Prokofiev, Asen Gavrilov, the main choreographer of the Sofia Opera, arrived in Chile for the production of *Giselle*. From his Bulgarian friends living in our hotel, Asen learned that, in Santiago, Chile, the famous Beryozka Dance Company had become stranded on their way to Argentina. This way Sasha Prokofiev found out about us, remembered that his school friend works in the ensemble, and decided to visit us in difficult times. For joy, we did not know where to invite them to sit and what to offer to eat (but there was nothing to eat anyway!). But Sasha had suspected our situation and had brought a bottle of wine and cookies.

And so, sitting in a modest hotel setting, Sasha Prokofiev, already having experienced in the Chilean life, began to talk about the situation in the country. We had accumulated a lot of questions! And he talked and talked. He told us about the arrests, raids, and searches of the houses of residents. He told us how the economic situation had become so difficult. He described how women had demonstrated with empty pots and pans in their hands because they had nothing to cook. He explained how all this had led to a military coup. Two hours passed quickly; Prokofiev had to leave, but he promised to come again.

The current situation is such that the external environment is normalizing. The hours during which people could walk around freely in the city are now expanded. People could be outside from 10:00 a.m. to 6: p.m.

On this Friday, there appeared a little hope that on Monday we would be able to fly to Buenos Aires. Our relatives in Moscow were probably already worried. We actually hoped that our relatives in Moscow were in the dark, thinking we were already in Argentina.

The Murder of President Allende

Also on this Friday, rumors began to circulate about the assassination of the Chilean president, Salvador Allende. These were rumors among the people; we heard not a single word in the press. But, oddly enough, different people were telling the same story, and the coincidence of details (of course, an accidental coincidence) was amazing.

So, what did the people say? During the storming of the presidential palace, the bodyguards and the secret service guarding the president could no longer contain the pressure of the regular army led by General Pinochet, and a young lieutenant burst into the president's office. Seeing President Allende in front of him with a weapon in his hands, he shouted, "Surrender! Lay down your arms!" President Allende, without shooting at the lieutenant, replied: "I am the president! Presidents don't give up. Lay down your arms!" And then, the enraged lieutenant shot the president. At that moment, a general ran into the president's office. Seeing President Allende killed, he shouted, "What have you done! We wanted to adjudicate him!" And, in a rage, he released the entire clip of his weapon at the lieutenant.

Thus, it turned out that the storming and ultimately victorious soldiers could not show the body of President Allende because it would be clear to everyone he had been murdered; they were able to show only something wrapped in a blanket.

The Coup, Day Five

On Saturday, September 15, it was announced that the curfew had been reduced by another hour. Now people can freely move around the city from 10 a.m. to 7:00 p.m. But that doesn't apply to us. We are still restricted by our documents and visas. To these problems was added another—air tickets to Argentina. The new authorities of Chile (the junta) opened the Santiago Airport, but diplomats from all countries accredited to Chile bought up all tickets for all flights for several days in advance. This is understandable; the diplomats need to fly to their countries to decide what relationships their countries would have with the new government of Chile. We just must sit and wait.

On television, normal Saturday broadcasts resumed. It is as if there has been no coup. Sasha Prokofiev visited again, this time with his wife, Julia, and their almost-three-year-old daughter, Nastya. Immediately, our hotel room took on such a homey atmosphere. We temporarily forgot about the coup, about the shooting. And when, after a while, we discovered that there really were no shots, Sasha Prokofiev, as an expert on local customs, authoritatively declared that, on Saturdays and Sundays, they did not fight. In addition, Sasha decided to support us; he brought another large bottle of local wine and some more cookies. So, with wine, conversation, and games with Nastya we passed the fifth day of our forced idleness.

The Coup, Day Six

On the morning of Sunday, September 16, we learned that the junta added yet another hour of free movement around the city. The curfew was now lifted from 10 a.m. to 8:00 p.m. It had also been announced that normal life and work will resume on Monday. Two trade unions, along with trade workers and truck owners, had announced on Friday that they were ready to go to work. Today, every five to ten minutes, radio stations broadcast their appeals to union members.

In the middle of the day, we hear shouts in the hotel: "The luggage has been brought! The luggage has been brought!" The airport authorities had decided to return our luggage to us; it had been stored since our arrival in Chile in a locked airport room. We, of course, hurried down to the hotel lobby and pulled our heavy suitcases to our rooms. After all, we had packed certain products as we prepared for a long trip from home: salami, canned stew, condensed milk. Some of us also had sweets. And we, for six days, had been existing on near-starvation rations at the hotel. The food we had packed was very much needed. We got knives from somewhere, and I cut a salami sausage. Finally, we were able to treat our guests as they sat traditionally in our room—Sasha Prokofiev and Asen Gavrilov.

Despite the local habit of not fighting on Saturdays and Sundays, shooting suddenly started somewhere near the hotel in the afternoon. It lasted for thirty to forty minutes and died down just as suddenly as it had begun. But we, already accustomed to shooting and rumble, did not even interrupt our meal and conversation with friends. Thus ended our sixth day in Chile.

The Coup, Day Seven

On Monday, September 17, life changed significantly. Lots of events happen all in one day. From early morning, we hear the noises of crowds of people in the streets, along with the sounds of cars and buses. In general, these are the sounds of a normal life. The junta announced that everyone must go to work today by 11:30 a.m.; otherwise, they would be fired or transferred to vacant positions. (I am trying to translate as closely as possible the official text of the junta's announcement on the radio).

Opposite the hotel, right in front of our windows, there is a grocery store. The crowd attempting to shop there was huge, and some people started fights as they stood in line. The authorities had to supply a soldier with a machine gun to regulate the line. This sobered the crowd and, to some extent, calmed them. What is the matter? We learned that there had been no meat or many other products in stores for a long time. And today, on the seventh day of the coup, the junta had organized the delivery of groceries to stores.

Unexpectedly, a five-minute readiness alert announced for us. Various versions of our possible departure from Chile had emerged. Maybe our dear Aeroflot representative, Vladimir Ivanovich, had been able to meet with the Chilean authorities as well as with the Consul of Argentina in order to obtain for us exit visas from Chile and entry visas to Argentina. And one more, absolutely incredible hope—maybe there would be tickets for some airline to accommodate ninety or so people who were eager to get to Buenos Aires. We sit on our suitcases ready to go. And so we sat all day.

The coup, day 3, Santiago. Chronicle Video on TV

The coup, day 3, Santiago. Chronicle Video on TV

The coup, day 7, Santiago. 09.17.1973

The Coup, Day Eight

Tuesday, September 18, is a national holiday in Chile. In fact, it is the most important holiday—Independence Day from the Spanish Crown.

Of course, nobody works. It is even useless to look for someone from the Chilean authorities. It is also useless to seek out the Argentinian consul. He is celebrating the Chilean holiday with the Chileans. And we continue to sit.

There is absolutely nothing to do in the hotel. We cannot leave the building. There are no books, and we are not able to bring books with us on a long trip because of the weight of the suitcases. Nothing serious is being shown on television. Even if one of us understand Spanish, watching the same cartoons for the tenth time had lost its charm, if there had been any to begin with.

But I found something to do. In the middle of the day, when everyone is busy with their own business, I put my ballet shoes in my pocket and went up to the roof of the hotel. Without changing into studio clothes, wearing my light ordinary clothes, I warm up with our usual ballet exercises on barre. Then, I jump a little. Pirouettes are impossible to do; the concrete surface of the roof is very rough. Thus, the combination of movements and jumps I can practice is limited. But it is enough to keep me fit. And it is necessary. I understand that someday our "confinement" in the hotel will end, the serious work will begin, and we must be ready to show our high level of art mastery.

Information is passing via word of mouth about our upcoming departure from Chile. Or, rather, about the impossibility of our departure. Moreover, this information is fact, not rumors. The information came from our dear Aeroflot representative, Vladimir Ivanovich, and was confirmed by our Beryozka management.

The first option was to accept the offer of the Chilean authorities to fly us on a Chilean plane. But, since Chile had turned overnight from a socialist country and a friend of the Soviet Union to become an enemy of socialism and the Soviet Union, our embassy and our government categorically prohibited this option. They were afraid of sabotage.

In addition, we had heard about cases of bad attitude toward the sailors of Soviet ships docked in the port of Santiago. From the Soviet press, through our embassy, we learned that the sailors had been thrown from the deck into the holds (and the depth of the hold is several floors).

The second option, also proposed by the Chilean authorities, was to transport the entire ensemble and all our luggage across the mountains to Argentina on several buses. Remembering the school buses that transported us from the airport to the hotel, and the others we had seen in Santiago, we knew that the journey would take several days. And realizing that there are no decent hotels or any kind of normal food in the mountains, we refused this option too. And, as it turned out later, we did the right thing. Many years later, in 1996, the Russian Seasons Dance Company traveled along this route for about half of the route proposed to us, from Santiago to the mountain town where they were supposed to perform. It took for them two days!

So, we continued to sit hopelessly in the hotel.

The Coup, Day Nine

What we did not expect that Chile's National Day would continue into a second day. On Wednesday, September 19, we were told that "such is the tradition in Chile". They celebrate their independence from the Spanish crown for two days. This was confirmed by the press. However, a workday had been announced. The streets are noisy. How a national holiday and work can be compatible is not clear.

Regarding our departure from Chile, we knew that our Aeroflot representative and our embassy were looking for the Argentine attaché to obtain permission for us to enter Argentina. But—and it was a big but—the calendar indicated that September 19 and 20 are the days of the National Day of Argentina. Nobody knows what this holiday is and what it means. But these days are marked as no-work days in Argentina, and the Argentinian Consul in Chile was celebrating this holiday with his people. You can laugh, but we had no desire for laughter. Every day was dear to us!

A two-minutes readiness alert announced for us. All suitcases and bags are already packed and secured. We, everyone, sit in our rooms. So we sat this way all day.

The Coup, Day Ten

On Thursday September 20, something wonderfully unexpected happened. The hotel administration opened the pool, which, it turns out, had been in working order all the time but had been closed. Sadly, we had been sitting in our rooms for ten days missing movements, unable to exercise! Immediately after breakfast, we all rushed into the pool.

Ours was one of the best hotels in the city of Santiago. The roof over the pool was retractable! Without leaving the hotel, we had the joyful opportunity to breathe the open air and sunbathe in the natural light of the sun!

With the opportunity to swim and take the sun at the pool, our confined life at the hotel became easier. We swim and sunbath as if we were at a fine resort! Our management asks us to start practicing, to get in shape. Everyone is skeptical about it. The dancers say there are nowhere with the proper conditions for taking exercise. But I already have my favorite place—the roof of the hotel, overlooking the city. Since no coup events are happening now, no one goes out onto the roof. I exercise in peace, unnoticed by anyone.

The Coup, Day Eleven

It is easy to quickly get used to good things. We quickly got used to the pool with its open roof through which we could hear the sounds of the city. We got used to the real hot South American sun, from which we ought to be careful, but we missed the sun and the fresh air while we were sitting inside the hotel for so many days.

On this, eleventh day of the coup, after a quick breakfast, we went down to the pool, took a dip, and relaxed, expecting a long day in "hotel confinement."

The soloist of the ensemble, the singer Victor Marchuk, suddenly runs into the pool area shouting in his well-tuned voice so everyone in the entire pool area hears him that, in twenty-five minutes, we are leaving! We should pack up and secure our belongings. We are going to the airport!

Nobody believes him. We all think it is a joke, a prank. Nobody moves. Marchuk becomes angry and shouts again, more persistently this time. But we notice something different. There is some sort of excitement in the hotel. People are running around. We become convinced. We throw ourselves into the water for the last time and then run to our rooms to collect our things. Twenty-five minutes? No - in ten minutes, the entire ensemble is downstairs with all their assorted suitcases and bags waiting for the buses to come. While we are waiting, the situation becomes clearer. It turns out that the Italian airline Alitalia kindly offered us seats on their flight to Buenos Aires. Moreover, they have room for everyone! We are so lucky!

Buses arrive at noon, we load. At this moments, two minutes before we were to depart, Julia and Nastya Prokofiev show up. (How did they know that we were leaving? That is still mystery.) Sasha is at work in the theater. But Julia believes that Sasha's contract will not last long and they would soon be leaving for Moscow. The authorities in Chile are no longer friendly to the Soviet Union.

Departure from the Hotel

All the hotel staff—all the maids and restaurant wait staff—came out to see us off. We had spent eleven days at the hotel, and such difficult and dangerous times had made us friends. But it is also important to realize that, after living for three years in a young socialist country with the socialist president Allende, they considered us brothers. Despite the devastation the country experienced under Allende, these workers looked at us—well-dressed and well-groomed world-class artists with the hope that their country would come to the same result someday. But now those dreams had collapsed, and no one knew what the future was for Chile with General Pinochet and the new government in charge.

(Looking ahead, I will say that General Pinochet took the tough but correct path of Chile's development. He returned the country to the mainstream of the world capitalist society and restored the country's economy. And after fifteen to twenty years, Chile began to be called the best country of the South American continent. But then, in 1973, no one knew this and could not assume anything about the future. Everything was unknown.)

At first, on each floor, as we carried our suitcases to the hotel lobby, maids stood along the corridor and warmly said good-bye with tears in their eyes. And when we started getting on the buses, all the hotel staff gathered on the balcony of the second floor. They waved their hands, almost crying. We found this touching. It was a heartfelt farewell on our part as well as theirs.

As we drive through the city, we notice that somewhat normal life had returned. We see many people on the streets, and all shops are open. There are long queues at grocery stores. Obviously, there had been no food for a long time.

We pass the back of the presidential palace La Moneda, not along the side from which the assault was shown on television. But on the back side, we see the same results of the battle—dark gray smoked walls. Broken glass in all windows of the palace made the windows look like gaping empty eye sockets.

As we travel further, we see people covering up the graffiti on the walls and scraping off paper ads. Everything is smeared: "Allende!" "Senator Valodia!" "No to fascism!" "No to civil war!"

Santiago Airport

Finally, we get out of the city traffic and rush at full speed to Santiago Airport. Our tension gradually lessens. Are we going to take off, hopefully?

And suddenly, a full stop!

The highway is blocked by wooden fences, and military men with weapons are stopping all cars. They examine the airline tickets of people who had them. They look through the travelers' luggage, opening suitcases right here on the highway, on the ground. Passengers with tickets and luggage are allowed onto special buses standing on the other side of the wooden fences. People had to drag their luggage themselves. Their escorts are sent back to the city; no one is allowed to pass. The soldiers allow through one car with a flag on the car that indicates diplomatic immunity!

Then, they decided to let us pass. We are forced to open our suitcases right here on the highway in front of the soldiers who are armed with machine guns. After looking through our luggage, the soldiers allow us to drag our suitcases onto special empty buses on the other side of the fence. We manage to get our suitcases into the buses. We must climb over them to sit down. Then, for another fifteen minutes, we endured the ride to the airport, shaking the entire way.

We finally arrive at the unusually empty Santiago Airport. Our group is immediately fenced off in the corner, guarded by two soldiers with machine guns. The customs procedure begin—luggage inspection again.

I believe that the search will be very thorough. But I have a few rolls of photographic film I had taken during the coup. What to do? I spoked in a whisper with several friends. I gave them each one roll of film so that the quantity would not be so noticeable. Thanks to my friends, my films made it out of the country.

The soldiers are looking in our luggage for weapons and for newspapers published before the coup. But we do not have any of this sort of things. Our flight is severely delayed. There are a lot of people leaving, and there are many formalities to do with their documents.

At four in the afternoon, we finally take off, four hours after having left the hotel with not a minute of respite. But now we can catch our breath on the Alitalia plane. We had escaped from the coup!

Late in the evening, at about ten o'clock, after a stopover in Montevideo, Uruguay, we land in Buenos Aires, the capital of Argentina. We are met by comrades from the Soviet Embassy, who immediately informed us that the Soviet government had broken off diplomatic relations with Chile at 4:30, exactly thirty minutes after our departure! If we had been delayed by some reason for thirty minutes, it was not known when we would have taken off or if we would have taken off at all.

But now, at the airport in Buenos Aires, there is nothing to be afraid of. A helicopter is circling over the airport, dropping leaflets. I catch one and astounded to see that it is about us! Large letters declare "BERYOZKA IS BACK!" And a story about our dance company written in such a way as to imply that Beryozka left for a little while and had finally returned home.

But that is another story. Which will start exactly from this point—from the landing in Buenos Aires.

ARGENTINA

*S*o, we are at the Buenos Aires airport. Friday, September 21. We received such a warm greeting. Lots of press are present, making our arrival an event: "BERYOZKA IS BACK!" In addition, Beryozka had not just arrived, they escaped from the hottest point on the planet! Our photos are taken, journalists interviewing our management team. But everything is on the go, as we heading to gather our luggage and board our buses.

Our impresario, Alfonso, is visibly pleased with our arrival. So far, he had endured continuous financial losses, which had begun the moment we were unable to take off from the capital of Chile on September 10. The Luna Park sports palace had been closed and empty. Alfonso had rented it for us, the ensemble, and paid a lot of money for every day of downtime. After all, this sports palace, like the Luzhniki Sports Palace in Moscow, accommodates from seven to twelve thousand spectators. A hotel in the central part of the city on the main street of Corrientes is also probably worth a lot of money. Well, at least he doesn't need to spend a lot on transport. Luna Park is located on the same street—Corrientes—a ten-minute walk apart. But to avoid any surprises, Alfonso gave us buses on the first day of our stay. Of course, it was very well thought out. Indeed, on the first day we needed to take a lot of things from the hotel to work. Later, when regular concerts were established, only one bus was waiting for us after the concert, for the dancers who were the most tired. Many of us preferred to walk and get some fresh air. In general, I have always noticed that no one appreciates fresh air as much as ballet dancers. This is understandable; after several hours of work in the dust and sweat of the rehearsal studio, fresh air is urgently needed!

But I digress. Let's return to the airport, where we are in a hurry to retrieve our luggage and get to the hotel as soon as possible to rest and get ready for the concerts. Despite our weariness, we are determined to start the concerts as soon as possible. Even the next day!

But it was not possible. Our comrades from the Soviet Embassy informed us that we would not be allowed to give concerts for political reasons. The first concert might not take place earlier than Tuesday of the following week. We had arrived on Friday. On Sunday in Argentina, there will be presidential elections—the first elections in eighteen years! Juan Domingo Perón, strikingly popular in Argentina, had been elected president of Argentina three times! He had served for nine years, from 1946 to 1955. And in 1955, Perón had been overthrown by the army. (Do you remember the coup in Chile, just eleven days ago? A similar story was for Argentina. It happens more or less regularly throughout the entire Latin American continent, almost in every country.) Perón had left the country and lived in other countries for eighteen years, but the country had not forgotten him. And in 1973, when one of the followers of Perón (they were called Peronists), Hector Jose Campora, was elected president of Argentina, he applied to Perón and offered him safe return to the country. Not only that, he proposed holding free democratic elections the way it had been eighteen years previously. The people greeted this idea with delight! And then we descended two days before the elections—a Soviet dance ensemble offering joyful, optimistic performances. The Argentine parliament decided that, if an ensemble from a socialist country could succeed (and success was inevitable), then the people of Argentina on Sunday would vote for the socialists, for the left. In order not to shake the scales of popularity, they decided that it would be easier to postpone the beginning of the performances of the super-popular ensemble for a while after the elections. It is sad, but we have to wait.

Upon arrival at the hotel, at midnight, a plan was drawn up and announced. Since concerts could not be held, we will hold a rehearsal on Saturday for ourselves. We need to get in shape. Elections are on Sunday. No one in the country would be working on election day, including workers at Luna Park, so we would have a mandatory day off. But, on Monday, we'll have a dress rehearsal wearing the costumes we would wear for the actual performance. This rehearsal will be open to the press. Their advance coverage will help attract more audience.

First Rehearsal on a New Stage

So, on Saturday, September 22, we finally entered the long-awaited empty Luna Park sports facility. The greeting by staff members was more than friendly! We were shown comfortable, clean dressing rooms and a good-sized stage. Everything was conducive to the desire to work, and work well. However, this stage presented some difficulties. There are no side wings. It means we have to change the entrance onto the stage at the beginning of our dances as well as our exit from the stage at the end. Furthermore, two of our dances—"Coachmen" and "Russian Souvenirs"—begin with the artists already on stage. We were used to the shelter provided by a curtain to bring them onto the stage and remove them from the stage after the dance, but there was no curtain here. An alternative plan will be to cut the lights, creating total darkness. Another dance—"Cossack Suite," about high-speed horse racing—also requires a change in the pattern of entering and leaving the stage. We have to work out these issues on this first day of rehearsal.

Presidential Elections

Sunday, September 23. We have a day off. The election of the president of the country is a serious matter in Argentina! No one should work. Everyone—and I mean everyone—must have the time and opportunity to come to the polling station and vote.

Taking advantage of free time, I left the hotel to wander around the city. I heard somewhere not far away voices from a loudspeaker. I walked toward the sound and ended up in a square crowded with people. I tried to see who was speaking from the rostrum. His spoke in a hot, temperamental, and fast South American tone, but where was he? People were standing tightly together; everyone tense in their attention to the speaker. There was nothing more interesting for me to see, and I did not know the city either. I decided to go back to the hotel.

At the hotel, as we were listening to the radio, at around three o'clock we learned that Perón had been elected president of Argentina. This had been expected, but somehow nervously expected. Perón was elected by a wide margin from other candidates (which, by the way, we had not heard anything about). He got 60 percent of the votes!

What had this news started? On the central street of Buenos Aires, where we were staying, there was a dense car demonstration. Cars moved slowly, all in one direction, occupying the entire roadway. They drove in tight formation, close to each other. And everyone was honking! Ta-ta, ta-ta-ta, ta-ta, ta-ta-ta! This sound of all cars still rings in my ears! The noise was terrible! In addition, when we saw an open truck, it would be full of people who stood, danced, jumped, and screamed at the same time! And an orchestra was playing! We had never seen such enthusiasm!

Of course, we had participated in our elections in the Soviet Union many times. All of us would be festively dressed, the official orchestras would be playing. But we all knew in advance who would be elected. No surprises were expected under a one-party system; there could not have been any. The Communist Party long ago, even at the time of the creation of the Soviet Union, declared (in the voice of Vladimir Lenin) that we did not need a second party. It would be useless to nominate any other candidates; the candidates from the Communist Party were superior to all.

We were surprised, even dumbfounded, by the enthusiasm we witnessed in Argentina. We lay across the windowsills, leaning from our waists out into the street. This went on hour after hour, and the enthusiasm of the people did not subside. As evening descended, morning arrived in Moscow. Our relatives woke up and started calling, looking for us and asking about Chile. Regularly, as soon as one of our people ran to either to the hotel lobby or to his room to talk to Moscow, his place on the windowsill was occupied by another, and this went on for hour after hour, until two in the morning! Not immediately, but gradually, the car demonstration faded away, and at around three, we were able to go to bed.

Murder and Mourning

On Monday morning, September 24, as we began to prepare for the rehearsal, we turned on the radio. What? They are talking about a murder! But what a murder—there is a celebration in the country. Perón is elected president! The details are gradually becoming clear. Immediately after the election of Perón, the leader of trade unions who helped Perón win the elections was killed. It was purely a political murder. *That is how the real true name of South America begins to appear - "a flaming continent."* As a consequence of the murder, a three-day mourning period had been declared in the country.

All entertainments are closed—theaters, cinemas, concerts— everything! This means that we will have to sit in the hotel without work for another three days. The only thing we were allowed to do was to hold a rehearsal in an empty sports palace. After a good, deep, detailed warm-up, selecting the costumes and putting on makeup, in the middle of the day we went on stage and began the performance we called for the press a "dress rehearsal." For all our performances, the hall layout option for seven thousand spectators had been chosen. So, in the auditorium set up for seven thousand people, sat a mere fifteen spectators, all journalists. But we had to dance, work, and smile as if the hall was filled. We danced, did tricks, and smiled so broadly, as if we saw seven thousand people before us!

But after the dress rehearsal, we returned to the hotel and again sat within four walls. Of course, we were not prohibited from leaving the hotel as we had been in Chile. In Argentina all our documents were in order. But we did not know the city and we hadn't earned any money yet so it was useless to think of going anywhere.

In the middle of the next day, Tuesday, September 25, we were given a small advance so we could buy food. We decided to gather in groups of four and put our money together. It would be easier to cook for small groups, and it would cost less to buy for four than to buy for one. In our group, the functions of treasurer and buyer of groceries were assigned to me. Because I could speak Spanish, I could explain what I needed. Knowing the language could also help me save money. So, I entered a small shop and stood in a long, slow-moving line. Everyone stood in silence; the situation was sad. An overweight, dark-skinned, elderly woman entered the store and immediately said indignantly from the doorway: "What a life this is! We live like in America!" Everyone silently swallowed her remark. We couldn't object; she spoke the truth.

So, sadly, these three days of mourning consumed everyone in the country. And for us, it was three more days of sitting in the hotel trying to occupy ourselves and trying to keep ourselves in shape, doing our dance exercises as we held on to a chair or a wall.

First Performance!

In joyful excitement, but also experiencing some anxiety, we came to our first concert. How will it go? It was the nineteenth day since we had flown from Moscow. Circumstances like the ones we have been experiencing now had never happened in the history of the ensemble. For nineteen days, we have been without regular daily classes, without rehearsals, without jumping and squatting. How will our bodies behave? Hopefully, the few recent rehearsals we had helped us to get it in some sort of shape. And the audience? Will they come, preoccupied as they were with the events that have taken place—the election of the president and the assassination of a political figure?

While we are making up, preparing our costumes, and warming up, the hall is empty. But half an hour before our performance is to begin, we look out through the back curtain into the stadium. The seats are gradually filling up, but we have no idea whether it would be full.

And now - we hear the first sounds of the orchestra introducing our round dance, "Birch." As we perform this first dance, we find out what kind of audience filled the hall. We count how many times the audience applauds during the first dance; this will show us what the mood is in the hall. Yes, we are convinced that our first Argentine audience is waiting for us! They like the round dance, and they are eager to see more and more dances. This inspires us, and we dance better and better. Each of us entering the stage through the darkness and blinding spotlights can see that the hall is full; there is not a single free space! The performance seems to take place in one breath.

After the Performance

We change out of our costumes after the concert and going out into the street through the stage entrance. There is a crowd waiting for us! It was impossible to determine how many people had gathered, but everyone is stretching out their hands offering programs for autographs! Multiple voices keep asking, "Habla usted español?" ("Do you speak Spanish?") All our people shake their heads—no. But I answered. "No tengo la menor idea" ("I have not the slightest idea"). There was a brief sad pause of reflection, and then a burst of laughter! A person who has fluently said such a phrase must speak Spanish! Everyone moved closer, and the conversation began with questions: Where are you from? From which city? Where did you learn to speak Spanish? Suddenly, I heard a timid voice speaking in Russian: "Can I talk to you?"

I instantly turned to the girl who asked this question. It had been unexpected and pleasant to hear Russian words in this ocean of Spanish language. They were a couple, a young woman, and a man about my age. The woman gently and delicately, in Russian, but with an accent, asked: "My mother could not go with us to the concert; she is sick. But she really wants to meet you. Would you agree to come to our house for dinner?" The Russian language in Buenos Aires is a rarity; it must be respected. Moreover, the mother of this woman was a sick person; she must be doubly respected. We exchanged glances with my friend Eugene Kudryavtsev, who was, by that time, standing next to me. Eugene and I shared a room together during all company tours. We asked ourselves if there was anything urgent that might interfere with this dinner plan, and we decided there wasn't; we could go to dinner with these strangers. "And we'll bring you back to the hotel," the woman added, to remove any doubts. We agreed.

Natasha and Andrey—our new acquaintances—invited us into their small car, and we drove off. It took a long time to drive along the dark streets; they lived far from the city center. On the way, we made one stop to buy dinner at the store. When Natasha asked us what we would like for dinner, we did not know what to answer, and not because we were not hungry. No, we were hungry after working hard at the concert. But in Moscow, at those years it would be impossible to buy ready-made and warmed-up food in a store; we just did not know that it was possible here in Argentina. Therefore, Natasha and Andrey purchased food at their discretion, and we drove on to their house.

We entered a small, neat apartment. Natasha's mother was in a wheelchair and, apparently, was unable to get up let alone come to our performance. We realized that we had made the right decision to visit her. Maria Mikhailovna was tall (as far as could be judged as she sat in her wheelchair) and thin. She said she was born in the previous century, in 1898, so now she was seventy-five years old. Maria Mikhailovna spoke intelligently in a soft voice. Her Russian was beautifully correct, something very rare in Russia at that time. She was very happy with our arrival, and as soon as we sat down on the sofa, while Natasha was laying the table, she began to question us with great interest.

Here is our conversation as I so vividly remember it:

"Where are you from, dear boys?"

"We are from Moscow."

"Oy, I am from Moscow too! Where do you live in Moscow?"

"I live on Komsomolskaya Square," I answered. Mom was not impressed by this; apparently, this name was not familiar to her. "This is a square with three railroad stations—Kazansky, Yaroslavsky and Leningradsky," I explained. Mom understood.

"Oh, that is interesting, I lived nearby. And you?" She turned to Eugene.

"I live on Novo-Basmannaya Street."

"And I lived on Novo-Basmannaya Street too!" She threw up her hands. Mom's surprise knew no bounds. "What house?"

"I live in house number ten."

"And our family lived in house number sixteen! My dear!"

I was completely forgotten. Maria Mikhailovna and Eugene gossiped with each other as neighbors, discussing the details of the people from their common street. Eugene and I, of course, knew house number sixteen. After all, we both (although in different years) studied dance at house number fourteen in the Central House of Children of Railway Workers. In this building was the pioneer song and dance ensemble, I must say, one of the best in Moscow, which had produced many well-known and even famous singers, musicians, and dancers. House number fourteen, the former home of a wealthy industrialist, Stakheev, was very large, with halls for choir and orchestra, and a ballet studio. House number sixteen was relatively small, surrounded by a high wall. It housed a diplomatic mission from some country, but we did not know which one.

So, unexpectedly, we met neighbors, but far away in Argentina, half the world from Moscow. Our friendship began that night with Natasha and her family, and this friendship continues today almost fifty years later!

Russians in Argentina

After supper, more conversations began. And, of course, our first question was how was it that we heard the Russian language spoken by Argentinian residents? And we were surprised to learn that there were a lot of Russians in distant Argentina! In Buenos Aires alone, there were three hundred thousand Russians, all trying to preserve Russian culture. Scout (in our language, pioneer) camps were created for children, where children spoke the Russian language and sang Russian songs. Which songs, we asked. And Natasha sang, "Hello, hello, dear potato-tato-tato-tato." She sang the entire song. We were dumbfounded. But Natasha continued, informing us that the Russians living in Buenos Aires gathered in a society, and this society subscribed to Soviet newspapers, which arrived more or less regularly. People knew what was happening in their historical homeland. When Argentina banned direct subscriptions from the USSR, members of the Russian group in Argentina found a Russian-Argentinian man working at customs, and they used him to subscribe to Russian newspapers through the United States. These newspapers arrived at a slower pace. The newspapers they subscribed to were gradually banned, and the list was reduced. As far as I remember, *Komsomolskaya Pravda* (*Youth Newspaper*) was the one that they received for the longest time. We in the USSR also loved this newspaper.

So, the evening we spent with Natasha's family passed very warmly. We returned to the hotel after midnight. Starting that evening, Natasha and Andrei, along with their friend Edward, came to see us often at the hotel and at our performances. We also accompanied them to Argentine tango evenings in small restaurants, which are plentiful in Buenos Aires. Many members of our troupe got to know them and accepted them warmly as their own friends.

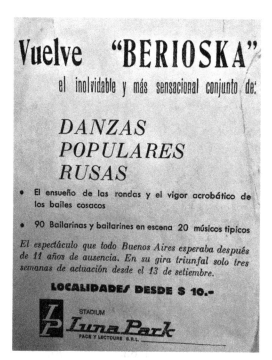

Leaflet in Buenos Aires, Argentina. 09.21.1973

First rehearsal in Luna Park. Buenos Aires, Argentina

Natasha de Zaikowski. Buenos Aires, Argentina

Andrey and Edik among dancers. Buenos Aires, Argentina

Moscow, Novo-Basmannaya, 14

Moscow, Novo-Basmannaya, 16

Work

And so the work in Argentina began! During the month we stayed there, we gave daily performances to a tight schedule: thirty performances in twenty-five days, which meant eight performances in six days with a day off, four days off total.

Eight concerts in six days! It was grueling work! We did three single shows on Tuesdays, Wednesdays, and Thursdays. And then there were concerts without a break other than a small gap between them. They were on Friday night, then on Saturday and Sunday, we gave two performances a day, one at two in the afternoon and one at eight in the evening. And, per order of our artistic director, as we called her, Madame Nadezhda Sergeevna Nadezhdina, only the main cast danced all performances; there were no substitutions. These were five concerts in a row without a breath between. And I had a lot of solos: "Coachmen," "Siberian Suite," "Balagurs" (the encore began from my solo in this one), and "Big Cossack Suite" (the encore began from my solo in this one too). In one dance, "Cossack Suite," I had five solo pieces, including a kozachok squat and an encore. When I went out for the encore after the kozachok squat on Sunday night—the last show of the week—I did not know if I would be able to finish the solo. I thought, *As it will be, so it will be.* But my legs held out! Plus, my smile helped. But when, on Monday morning, Eugene Kudryavtsev and I got out of bed, our legs were no longer holding. Because we shared a room, we saw how the work reflected on each of us. He also had a lot of solo jumps throughout our performance. On that morning, we moved around the hotel room holding onto the wall!

Our impresario, Alfonso, helped us as best he could. He ordered sandwiches in between double gigs, ordered juice for each dancer, and personally made sure everyone got "reinforcements." He even ordered a massage therapist who helped those who needed urgent care or fast recovery. We became good friends with him!

Days Off

Alfonso was good natured. He had attentive eyes and was always ready to listen and always ready to smile. He knew and remembered each member of our group of ninety people. He may not have remembered our names, but he remembered what each of us did on the trip. And not only what we did, but how we did it. He attended every performance and watched our dances very carefully. Amazingly enough, Alfonso remembered everyone! When a group of our artists met him in Moscow seven or eight years later, during our conversation, he named two dancers whom he remembered working to their fullest, with dedication during every performance regardless of the mood, the circumstances, and the fatigue. The first he mentioned was our soloist, Lena Suchkova. The second Alfonso mentioned was me.

But his main help and care for us happened during our days off. Knowing how important a steam room and body warming are for dancers, he allowed us to visit the bathhouse at his expense. So, every Monday morning, we, as a team of friends, went to the bathhouse, a large, five-story building with several steam rooms, a swimming pool, a massage area with young women masseuses, a small gym with dumbbells and barbells, a special floor for quiet relaxation, and a bar. We paid and then brought Alfonso our receipts; he always reimbursed us accurately.

And then the excursions ordered for us by Alfonso would begin. The first was a nature excursion to the Paraná Delta. The Paraná is a river in South America, the second longest river on the continent after the Amazon. It flows in the southern part of the continent through Brazil, Paraguay, and Argentina before reaching the Gulf of La Plata on the Atlantic Ocean near the city of Buenos Aires. We got a great breath of fresh air during a few hours of sailing on a small catamaran. We saw the immense expanse of the Paraná Delta and almost entered the Atlantic Ocean.

The next weekend we were treated to a trip to the traditional Argentinean restaurant, Gaucho, named after the famous Argentine horsemen and cowhands. As we were treated to wonderful Argentine food—meat, vegetables, and juices—the wonderful Argentine singer Horacio Guarany sang for us. A large man with a lion's hair, he sang Argentine folk songs. He was the most popular performer of folk songs in Argentina. During some of the songs, Horacio accompanied himself on the guitar, still managing to gesticulate as if helping to convey the meaning of the song. And when he was accompanied by a guitarist, Horacio gestured constantly; he even danced, tapping with his boots! His boots were so familiar to us; we performed in the same boots. All his songs were like a conversation with us, with the audience. Horacio also spoke between songs. It was a pity that we could understand little. Only the Argentines sitting around laughed.

On another weekend, our Soviet Embassy invited us to rest at the embassy's dacha outside the city, in nature. It was a fairy tale! There was Argentinean meat and Argentinean polo, and the traditional gaucho dance with stones. We called these stones eggs because of their shape: in Spanish, *huevos*.

In return, we would perform our skit, which was famous among the teams of performers of Moscow. The soul and inspiration of the skit was Viktor Temnov, our composer, accordion player, singer, and artistic director of the Beryozka orchestra. He came up with scenes, selected famous music so that it was easy to learn, and wrote his own humorous poems for this famous music. We had such scenes as the "Greeting of the Pioneers" (standard in those years throughout the Soviet Union), "Adagio, and the Dance of the Little Swans" (you cannot do anything without the classics), the "Gypsy Camp" (a tribute to the popular but well-worn genre), sometimes the famous "Canio" aria from the opera *Clowns* was included. It was performed wonderfully by our singer of the ensemble, Viktor Marchuk. We all took part in the skit with inspiration and put our strength and invention into jokes and acting. Our performance at the Soviet embassy turned out to be memorable. We had a very good rest that day!

In the evening, we also had time to watch the Argentinean tango show in the fashionable Karina Tavern. And after returning to the hotel, we also saw the famous jazz musician Carlos Santana's concert on television! It was a very rich day!

Adios, Argentina!

So our performances continued. It was hard work, and we gave out countless autographs after concerts. But we also spent time with the families of Natasha and her husband Andrey, and we took walks in the evening through Buenos Aires. We took some of our favorite walks along the fashionable Florida Calle, which had been closed to auto traffic just recently, in 1971. It was full of pleasant lighting from houses and fashionable shops. On Florida Calle, there is no asphalt; rather, there are tiles with beautiful colorful patterns. Since this street had only recently become a walking street, it was a new experience for our Argentinian friends as well.

On our very last day in Argentina, in the evening after the last concert, we were lucky to see the gaucho dancers in a small restaurant in Buenos Aires.

During this month, we got to know Argentinean people quite well. We learned that people of Argentina were a varied mixture from different countries of Europe. Many had run from fascist Germany when Hitler came to power. Fewer people had escaped from Stalin's influence in the USSR. We also met people who had been captured by the Germans during the war and had decided not to return to the USSR, knowing that a prison camp awaited them. From every country, the Argentines accepted the best aspects of character. From Germany, punctuality; from France, gallantry, manners, and the love of cheese (cheese in Argentina is added to many dishes and even to soups); from Italy, the love of and talent for music and devotion to big families. Other countries had added more value to Argentinian life.

On October 21, exactly one month after arriving in Argentina, we, tired but satisfied, flew to our next South American country, Peru. But Argentina had become, it was possible to say, a second home to us, and the Argentines had become like a part of our family.

Beryozka, Picnic. Buenos Aires, Argentina

Beryozka, Picnic. Buenos Aires, Argentina

Beryozka, Picnic. Buenos Aires, Argentina

Composer Victor Temnov always in the center
of attention. Beryozka, Picnic

Beryozka, Picnic

Beryozka, Picnic. Leonid Shagalov with a
representative of Soviet Embassy

Beryozka, Picnic. Comic performance 'Pioneers'

Beryozka, Picnic. Comic performance 'Swan Lake'

Beryozka, Picnic. Comic performance 'Swan Lake'

Beryozka, Picnic. Comic performance 'Gypsies'

Beryozka, Picnic. Comic performance 'Gypsies'

Beryozka, Picnic. Comic performance 'Gypsies'

Poster of 'Tango Karina' Cafe

Poster of 'Tango Karina' Cafe

PERU

*O*n Saturday, September 22, 1973, we flew out of Argentina. It was the day after our last performance. Checkout from the hotel was in the middle of the day, so we had the opportunity to rest a little and calmly pack. We arrived at the airport two hours before our departure. Check-in and luggage check went smoothly, and our plane took off at six o'clock on time. From Buenos Aires, Argentina, which is located on the Atlantic coast, we flew to the capital of Peru, the city of Lima, which is located on the Pacific coast. This journey took nine hours! South American airlines use mainly small aircraft, most often the Boeing 737, and international flights between Latin American countries are more like intercity bus journeys. We made two landings and, without leaving the plane, took off in again in twenty to thirty minutes each time. Much of our flight was after dark, so we slept most of the way.

Lima

We landed at three in the morning, our bodies deep in sleep. Still groggy, we dragged our luggage to the buses. In the same sleepy state, we arrived at our hotel and, without unpacking our luggage, collapsed into our beds. Now our task was to sleep fast, since the first performance in Peru was to be that night in the city theater in the center of the city. That means that entire government will be there to see our first show. This is a tradition that has never been broken, and we—ready or not——needed to be in good shape.

Performances

We gave our first two performances in a beautiful but small city theater. And then on a specially designated day off, we moved our production to the Dibos Coliseum. The stadium is truly colossal and unusual. As we approached the stadium, we did not see the building and the stands. The entire stadium was in a huge pit. The upper stands were at street level; we had to go down to the stage, into the pit, along a simple, dusty, unpaved road. A wooden stage had been specially built for us on the football field. Not only was it not a very comfortable stage; in some places, it was even dangerous for our legs because it was made of wooden planks. And it was small! Even though the space accommodated an entire football field, the organizers of the concert had decided to limit themselves to a small area. *The poor spectators!* we thought. But we could not tell the owners what to do; they had done what they thought was right, and we had to accept the venue as it was.

And, so, the work began! On our first day at the stadium, Friday, we gave one performance. Then, on Saturday and Sunday, we gave two performances each day, just as we had done in Argentina. After that, on Monday, we gave another performance. On Tuesday we were scheduled to fly to the next country. We performed six times in that stadium.

Thievery!

When we were at the hotel, we were interested in what to see in the city of Lima. People at the hotel advised to see a local attraction—the market. We shrugged our shoulders - what a strange sight! It is not a museum, not a theater. They explained to us that it was a permanent market, like a shopping center. It was a modern building made of glass and concrete. It housed shops, stalls, and individual private sellers. On our first day free from performances, we went into the city and found the market. Well, since there is nothing more interesting, will go to the market. The mood rose when we had been given our salary for the whole week, and we felt a kind of obligation to spend some money. But we had been warned to be careful; theft was rampant in the city. It was both professional and widespread; one might say, it was on a grand scale. Unfortunately, we found this to be true on our outing to the market.

When we traveled, we usually did our sightseeing in groups in order to protect ourselves and watch each other. On this trip to the market, we all walked together and kept our hands in the pockets of our tight jeans to protect our money. Most of us carried our entire week's salary. As we made our way through the crowd, at one place, our group of involuntarily split up. No one noticed how a group of local, seemingly friendly guys surrounded one of our guys, Yurka. One of the locals, as if it were accidental, stepped on his foot. Another, also as if it were an accident, pushed him slightly, but just enough to make Yurka lose his balance. To keep himself from falling, he pulled his hand out of his jeans pocket. Instantly someone else's hand slipped into that same narrow pocket. His entire week's salary slipped away into the hand of a thief. Only the polite

"*Perdoneme*" ("Excuse me") remained in the air. The entire group of local "friendly" guys instantly disappeared into the crowd. Later, at the hotel, we, analyzed this episode second by second, and realized how carefully this "performance" had been rehearsed.

The next day, a more serious incident happened. Maya, the ensemble tutor, was walking along one of the central streets of Lima with her husband, a musician in our orchestra. There should have been no danger. It was daytime, and this was the capital city of the country! Suddenly, right there on the sidewalk, Maya was overtaken by a motorcyclist traveling at high speed. Without stopping, the rider reached out with a razor and cut off the strap of her shoulder bag. The motorcyclist expected that the cut bag would fall into his hands by itself, but he was surprised to find it was not there! Russian women do not just give up their handbags! Maya had been holding her shoulder bag very tightly! The motorcyclist did not let go of her purse either. He began to fall and, as he fell, his motorcycle ripped into Maya's side. With blood flowing, she was taken by ambulance to the city hospital. She underwent surgery, and we did not see her for several days. Maya returned to the hotel only on the last day, just before we were due to leave for the airport. She was pale and thin from blood loss and from being hospitalized in a foreign country where she did not know the language.

The Stage is Crumbling!

But back to work at the stadium. The conditions under which we prepared for the performances and rested between double performances were the most primitive and unpretentious. And no matter how hard our impresario Alfonso tried, he could not change anything. We were somehow able to overcome the inconvenience. But, during the last performance, on Monday, we felt the stage began to rock. The wooden planks beneath our feet began to move! It happened during "Siberian Suite," a massive number that we performed right before intermission. Almost everyone in the entire ensemble was on stage; the weight load on the planks was at maximum! As the stage shook, all the men who did not dance on stage—stage workers; the technical director, Fyodor Ivanovich Shestakov; the lighting designer, Georgy Shustrov (a former dancer himself); the tutor, Vladimir Alekseevich Yakushin—all squatted under the stage and held up the bouncing wooden boards with their hands! We practically danced on the arms of our friends, not knowing what would happen the next minute. Somehow, with artificial smiles on our faces, we danced the "Siberian Suite" to the end.

During intermission, Fyodor Ivanovich, and after him, all the men who were not engaged in dancing, climbed under the stage. It was urgent that, during the intermission, they somehow secure the loose wooden boards. The dancers stood around watching, worried whether they would be able to continue the performance and bring it to an end. Just as intermission was coming to an end, Fyodor Ivanovich, and then all the others involved in the repair of the stage, crawled out from under the stage. Fyodor Ivanovich, small and nimble, without saying anything, ran to prepare the next dance, "Coachmen." He did not like to talk at all; maybe he was shy. But most importantly, he was a man of action. We rushed after him. "Well, can we work?" someone shouted at him. "Dance, dance!" Fyodor Ivanovich muttered as if we were boring him with our unnecessary questions. He absolutely did not want to portray himself as the hero of the day.

With fear in our hearts and smiles on our faces, we finished the concert to the end. The stage rocked and trembled under our feet, but it held fast. Only after the last bows as we impatiently listened to the applause of the admiring and unsuspecting spectators did we breathe freely.

The next day we flew to the next country, Venezuela.

Beryozka, Siberian Suite. Korolev, Shagalov, Ganiev

Beryozka, Jokers. Leonid Shagalov

Beryozka, Siberian Suite. Bear - Victor Marchuk

Beryozka. Gusev, Shestakov, Shustrov

VENEZUELA

*O*n October 30, 1973, we traveled from Peru to Caracas, the capital city of Venezuela (what a beautiful name) with a short stop somewhere in Colombia.

We had one day off before our performances began on November 1, and our schedule was similar to our previous one: a performance each on Thursday, Friday. Then, two performances on Saturday, and two performances on Sunday. And one performance each of Monday, and Tuesday. On Wednesday we were scheduled to fly to our next country. It was a heavy schedule, but we were used to the work; we had already become dancing machines.

We were amazed by the energy of Caracas. The streets were packed with cars; most of them were large. Gasoline was cheap because Venezuela produces and sells a lot of oil. There were a lot of people on the streets and a lot of goods in the shops.

Rear Admiral Rudnev

We discovered that there was also a Russian community in Venezuela. It had been formed at the beginning of the twentieth century by the families of Russian aristocrats who fled Russia during the 1917 Russian Revolution. Some had left long before the revolution, in 1912 and 1913.

We were told that the family of the middle son of the captain of the famous cruiser *Varyag*, Rear Admiral Rudnev, lived in Caracas. Rudnev was a hero of the Russo-Japanese war who sank his ship rather than surrender it to the Japanese. For the heroic battle in which the *Varyag* fought with six-times superior forces of the Japanese and sank two enemy ships, Rear Admiral Rudnev was awarded both Russian and Japanese orders. In 1905, Vsevolod Fyodorovich Rudnev received the Order of St. George from the Russian emperor. And in 1907, the Japanese emperor, in recognition of the heroism of Russian sailors, sent Rudnev the Order of the Rising Sun (which he accepted but never wore).

Rear Admiral Rudnev died in 1913, but his widow and three children left Russia in 1917 and reached France through Yugoslavia. From there, the middle son, George, emigrated to Venezuela. Some of our dancers were fortunate enough to meet these interesting people and listen to their stories. They even maintained friendship with George's family for many years, and George came to Moscow at their invitation.

Separated Brothers

Two days earlier, after our last performances in the stadium in Lima, Peru, as we approached our buses, we had been surrounded by a group of people wishing to get our autographs as souvenirs of a show they had enjoyed. This group was not as big as the group we had met in Argentina, but still, we were pleased at their positive reaction to our work. After I had given several autographs and had several conversations in Spanish, I heard a request in Russian, with an accent: "Sign, please!"

Before me stood a tall young man, very visible in the Peruvian crowd. "With pleasure!" I said, and I signed his program. We engaged in a short conversation, but there was no more time. "What is your name?" I asked.

"I am Peter."

"What is your work?"

"I am a firefighter," Peter answered. *That is logical, with such growth*, I thought. And then we were called to the bus. Peter and I quickly said good-bye. I jumped on the bus and waved to him.

Now, after our first performance in the city of Caracas, Venezuela, two days after our performance in Peru, we were again surrounded by a group of people wishing to get our autographs. Everything was going along as usual, but after several signatures and conversations in Spanish, I heard a request in Russian, with an accent: "Sign, please!"

Before me stood a tall young man, very visible in the crowd of Venezuelans. I had never seen this young man before, but the voice—I could not be wrong, I knew this voice! "What is your name?" I asked as I signed his program.

"Nikolai."

"Do you have a brother Peter in Peru?"

The young man's jaw dropped; he could not utter a word. "How do you know?"

We were already being called to get on the bus. "I saw him two days ago!" I called out as I ran and jumped onto the bus.

I had already heard stories from our Russian immigrants about how Russian families had moved across South America and around the world in search of better lives. Life was not easy, and often, after living for several years in one country and feeling that life was not going the way they wanted, a family would pack up and go to explore another country. Or one of the family members took a risk and went one to another country "for exploration." Perhaps the same story happened with the brothers Peter and Nikolai.

But I think about another strange side of this story. How small should be the chance that two brothers from two different countries stood in two different crowds of people who wanted to get autographs from artists, and both came to me out of ninety members of our group? I think the chance was negligible, but it happened! And I am very glad and remember for many, many years how I unexpectedly united the two brothers through their love for Russian art.

Caracas, Venezuela

Caracas, Venezuela

Caracas, Venezuela

Colombia, Bolivia, and Ecuador

Concerts with Security

The next three countries—Colombia, Bolivia, and Ecuador—between November 7 and November 13, 1973—flashed by like lightning, and we remember them mostly because of the number of security agents around us at all times. In the first country, Colombia, we were warned that people were being kidnapped, especially Europeans. We did not go out into the city during our stay there; nobody wanted to be kidnapped. Fortunately, I was able to purchase some of the famous Colombian coffee, which I really wanted to bring to Moscow, from a shop right in the hotel, and I calmed down once I had made this purchase.

But in the evening, we had to go to the theater, which was located only three to five hundred meters from the hotel. But we were told it was dangerous to walk even that short distance alone. It was announced that we would all walk to the theater together in a group. As soon as all the artists gathered in the hotel lobby, we were surrounded by more than twenty security agents wearing civilian clothes; they did not wear special uniforms. Thus, surrounded by guards, we walked to the theater. We walked right in the middle of the street; there was no car traffic. When we reached the theater, we went inside to get ready for the performance, and the guards took control of all the theater entrances, especially the service entrance behind the stage.

But the problem remained—how would we get back to the hotel? Some members of the group were only in the first part of the performance, so they were ready to go during intermission, but most of the dancers, as well as the entire orchestra, were busy until the end of the concert. We decided in this way: the artists who finished earlier than the others gathered in groups of five to eight people and, accompanied by two agents, went back to the hotel. No one went unaccompanied, it was strictly forbidden. The rest of us were similarly guarded when we returned to the hotel at the end of the performance.

This sort of behavior did not seem very strange to us. We had already encountered such cases on a tour to the United States the previous year. The rules were even stricter there. In those cities where there was a need for protection, we were guarded by uniformed policemen carrying firearms and batons. It is noteworthy that they did not sit during the concert. They stood throughout the concert, with their backs to the stage and did not look at the stage. They surveyed the public, looking for unexpected activities or even attacks from members of the public. After the concert, the police did not leave after seeing us to the hotel. They sat on all floors where the artists lived, controlling the entrance to the floor and did not sleep all night. That was security!

But just as we experienced in Colombia, guards surrounded us in Bolivia and in Ecuador. In Ecuador there were fewer guards, in fairness I must say. This meant that the situation in the country was calmer. In each of these countries, we gave only one performance, so our time there flashed by very quickly.

In the capital of Ecuador, the city of Quito, which is located at an altitude of 2,850 meters above sea level, oxygen machines were installed in the wings of the theater in case anyone in our company suffered from oxygen starvation. But nobody needed them. It is strange, however, that, in the capital of Bolivia, La Paz, which is much higher, at an altitude of 3,600 meters above sea level, there were no oxygen machines. Anyway, we danced without noticing the altitude.

Simon Bolivar

In every country, people tried to show us monuments to Simon Bolivar. And in one of these countries, despite the lack of free time, we managed to approach a monument dedicated to this young general. Simon Bolivar, a Venezuelan by birth, received an excellent education in Spain and France during his youth. Armed with the ideas of the Enlightenment, Bolivar returned to his native Venezuela, and from the age of twenty-five, he began to fight for the liberation of Gran Colombia from Spanish rule. At that time, the territory in the northern part of South America, equal in size to the entire area of Western Europe, was called Gran Colombia. Six countries now comprise this territory: Venezuela, Colombia, Peru, Ecuador, Panama, and Bolivia, which is named after Bolivar.

To achieve the independence of Gran Colombia, Simon Bolivar spoke at rallies throughout the country, participated in a hundred battles, and rode 70,000 kilometers (nearly 44,000 miles!) on horse-back. And when he achieved his goal and Gran Colombia gained independence from Spain, he became its first president—at the age of thirty-four! After that, he served as president of Bolivia, president of Peru, and several times president of Venezuela. In each country, he established a parliament and built the entire political system.

Simon Bolivar's battles and travels on horseback throughout Gran Colombia put him on a par with the great conquerors of the past—Hannibal, Napoleon, and Alexander the Great. However, the difference was that they were conquerors, and he was a libera-tor. That is why, in all countries of South America, Simon Bolivar is considered the Father of the Nation, and he bears the title of *El Libertador* (The Liberator).

A Change of Plans

On November 11, 1973, our tour of South America was com-ing to an end. We had one more performance, but we were already packing our bags in preparation for our flight to Moscow when, suddenly—*so many things happen unexpectedly!*

Before the concert, it was announced to us that plans were changing. We were not going back to Moscow right away.

COSTA RICA (A SURPRISE!)

*O*ur dance company received an order from the Ministry of Culture in Moscow. At the request of the Soviet Embassy in Costa Rica, we are to give several performances in San Jose, the capital of Costa Rica. Elections are coming up there, and in order to help the democratic forces—the left—win the elections, officials at the USSR Embassy want to organize our performances, which are full of optimism and energy. We had experienced the exact same situation in Argentina. There the government had feared our influence on the elections. And in Costa Rica, it seems that our embassy was able to convince the local government that it was safe to influence the election results with our dancing.

Well, an order is an order. In addition, we are pleased to participate in the political life of the country. We are learning what it is like to live the local life, even if indirectly. The next day, November 13, we flew north to Central America, to a tiny, warm country sandwiched on a narrow isthmus between North and South America, between Nicaragua and Panama. Costa Rica, we were told, was the *dacha*—seasonal second home—for Americans, where they usually fly for a short break to warm up during the cold season in the United States.

This flight from Ecuador to Costa Rica was not an easy one. At 4:30 in the morning, in a sleepy state and in the pitch dark, we checked out of the hotel, pulling out our suitcases, which had become heavier during the trip. By six we were already in the air and sleeping sweetly under the monotonous hum of a Boeing 737, a plane we had become accustomed to. An hour and a half later, we landed at the airport, which on Russian maps is spelled with two errors in one short word: Jujuy. (It was an intentional misspell to avoid association with a bad word).

San Jose, Costa Rica

We thought we had been required to fly out so early to accommodate an aggressive performance schedule but, when we landed in San Jose, the capital of Costa Rica, we learned we would have three days off—no rehearsals, no performances. The venues for our performances were not prepared. When we arrived for the afternoon rehearsal in the central square of Costa Rica after three days off, we heard hammering. The stage was being built before our eyes. The wings were hung up during our rehearsals, and workers, ignoring the dancers for whom the stage was being built, walked through the entire space of the stage, right through the dance pattern. The ballet tutors shouted at them in a mixture of languages: "Niet walking on the stage. Niet!"

We entered this stage with caution, still remembering the crumbling stage in Peru. We carried out the rehearsal casually without even changing into costumes. Local people just walked around us on the street.

Performances

The performances began on the same day. Since the city was not ready for us, we danced at different venues. The first performance was on an open stage, which was being built before our eyes. The second performance was at the National Theater of Costa Rica. Then we moved to the city gymnasium and gave three performances there in two days. And finally, the last performance again at the National Theater.

The Last Performance

The final performance of any tour is always very important for us. It is like a summing up, and we are excited with the anticipation of returning home to family. It is also a subconscious understanding that, on that day, we could spend every last bit of energy without thinking about performing the next day. All the artists dance with particularly high spirits and emotions.

This "last performance" today was no different. In "Siberian Suite," the bear, whose role was brilliantly played by the soloist singer Viktor Marchuk, amused the audience in a particularly funny way, tumbling on stage and doing his bear tricks and jumps. In the "Coachmen," Volodya Markelov, while doing squats with jumps and throwing his legs forward, instead of moving forward diagonally, began to jump backward, which is much more difficult, but he did everything correctly and cleanly.

At the last orchestral chord at the end of the "Big Cossack Dance," the entire ensemble—all the dancers on stage and everyone

behind the curtains—exhaled and shouted *"Vseo!"* ("That's it!")
Every audience in every country, even not knowing the language,
feels this emotional explosion and, in response, explodes with applause and a standing ovation to the beat of the music, and this continues until the very end of our "horseback riding" to the backstage
area. This is a tradition, and it is sacredly observed, passing from
generation to generation from older artists to younger artists.

Backstage and onstage, after we take our final bows and the curtain closes, everyone hugs and congratulates each other on the end
of the tour. Every tour is difficult, but this one had been especially
difficult, and moreover dangerous.

Tomorrow, we have a free day, and the day after that, on
November 22, we will fly to our homeland. To home! It will be a
long, long and, I think, grueling journey with several stops before
we land in Moscow. We were very fortunate to have a free day before
the flight home when we could safely pack our luggage, which had
increased on our way through several countries in Latin America. I
thought it would be nice to have another bag, so I went to the market
since it was not far from the hotel.

First, I immediately noticed how many American tourists there
were in the market. This confirmed what we had been told—Costa
Rica was a destination for Americans who wished to escape the cold
winter season. It was easy to spot the neatly dressed Americans.
English was spoken everywhere, and somehow automatically I was
drawn to speak English, which I knew a little after a tour in the
United States the previous year.

Passing the stalls, I noticed a sporty over-the-shoulder bag and
decided to ask the price. Like everyone around me, I asked the
question in English: "How much?" The saleswoman told me the

price in local currency. I mentally counted it into dollars. It turned out $14. I knew approximately the range of prices for such bags, and $14 seemed to me such a large amount that I (again automatically) switched to Spanish and asked again for the price: "Cuánto es esto?" The woman's face showed a little fright, and she named the price equal to $7 dollars. It was a fair price. I instantly paid the sales-woman, and for myself I concluded that using the local language is not only pleasant, but also profitable!

Siberian Suite

Siberian Suite. Bear Hunting

Siberian Suite. Choir

Siberian Suite. Men's Choir

Siberian Suite. Bear - Victor Marchuk

Siberian Suite. Bear - Victor Marchuk, Assistant - Tkach

PART 2

At Home between Tours

THE FLIGHT HOME

*O*n November 22, we left for home. We would have to take several flights before we landed in Moscow. The longest flight was from the capital of Mexico, Mexico City, to Paris. We flew on an Air France Boeing 747, an amazing airplane. For several decades, it was the largest airplane in the world!

There are many interesting things about this plane. I remember, a couple of years before our South American tour, our group landed in Singapore. Our plane stood next to a 747 as the passengers disembarked. We watched an endless line of people; it was like a demonstration! More and more people kept walking off the plane—434 people from one plane!

The Boeing 747 is a two-story plane. The cockpit and seating for first-class passengers are on the second level. Passengers from the lower cabin are not allowed there. Due to its large size and weight, the Boeing 747 flies very smoothly and calmly. Even the strongest wind cannot shake it.

A design competition announced by the United States government and Pan American Airlines in 1964 received submissions from Douglas, Lockheed, and others aircraft manufacturing companies, but Boeing surpassed everyone with the audacity of their design.

Their 747 would take on board the largest number of passengers ever, which translated into cheaper operations. This settled the matter.

To assemble this enormous aircraft, a building larger than any that ever existed was required. And Boeing built this building; at that time, it was the largest building in the world. The design and assembly of the aircraft took four years, and in 1968 the first Boeing 747 took off. For fifty-two years, Boeing has been producing this aircraft, which has become one of the longest-lived aircrafts in aviation history. Even now, in 2023, as I write these lines, Boeing plans to build fifteen more 747s. It is surprising!

But this aircraft can also be called amazing because the designers made this aircraft easily modifiable in appearance and purpose. This 747—passenger, cargo, and military plane— has extinguished fires, and taken the Space Shuttle into the stratosphere, from where it was easy for Shuttle to start its independent space flight. It is no coincidence that the Boeing 747 became the presidential aircraft, Air Force One. After all, it is possible to create excellent working and living conditions in it. Not many people know that, in a case of an attack on the United States, the presidential Boeing 747 takes the president on board and flies off in an unknown direction. Practically, it can fly a very long time with a refueling. And the US President, who is also the commander-in-chief of the US Army, becomes invulnerable to the enemy while at the same time retaining the ability to lead the army and the country. This was exactly the scenario that happened on September 11, 2001, when terrorists attacked the United States and destroyed the Twin Towers in New York. The presidential Boeing 747 lifted US President George W. Bush into the air and carried him away in an unknown direction. And when, a few years ago, the presidential Boeing 747 was in San Francisco during the

Fleet and Aviation Week, this plane made such tricks over the bay that other aircraft could not do. It was just breathtaking!

Moreover, Boeing's designers created the aircraft in such a way that, despite its gigantic dimensions and high flight speed (560 miles per hour), it does not need a special landing strip; it fits into a regular strip.

As a passenger plane, the Boeing 747 has undergone numerous modifications. Starting with the first version, which carried 366 passengers, the designers gradually came to eighth version, which carries 434 passengers. The flight speed also increased from 500 to 560 miles per hour, and the flight range increased from 5,600 to 9,000 miles.

And on such an amazing plane we had a chance to fly from Mexico City to Paris. The flight lasted ten hours. For a dancer who is accustomed to movement, it is very difficult to sit in a chair for ten hours. When I got tired of reading, I went for a wander on the plane. It turned out that, by this time the French flight attendants had already fulfilled their duties feeding and watering all the passengers, they were happy to have the opportunity to chat with an artist of the Russian dance company for whom the French language was not an obstacle. (I had studied French at the ballet school, like all future ballet dancers. I was a good student, and already at the school age I began to use French in the international pioneer camp Artek as a translator for a delegation of scouts—pioneers from Switzerland). I settled with some of the flight attendants at the end of the salon. I was sitting on the arm of the chair, so I was not wearing a seatbelt. The flight attendants also were not wearing seatbelts. We could see fog out the windows, a solid white shroud. During the conversation, we all missed the pilot's announcement that we were descending and it was time to fasten our seat belts. Of course, from time to time, I looked through the windows, but outside the windows, there was still the same white veil, and it was soothing. Suddenly, the plane jolted as it hit the ground, and the plane taxied along the strip of the airfield. It turned out that the fog went down to the very ground! It was so dense that we could not even see the wings of our plane and, of course, nothing around us. But for the Boeing 747, such a dense fog was not a hindrance. This plane had very sophisticated instruments for blind flight. And when we got off the plane, we learned that a Soviet Tupolev Tu-134 jet from Moscow had flown in for us, but he was not allowed to land because of the fog. The Tu-134 circled over the airport and flew back to Moscow.

After a short period of uncertainty, it was announced to us that the airline would provide us with hotel accommodation near the airport. This was an unexpected surprise for us as well as for our families who were waiting for us at home. But nothing could be done; no one can change the weather. We loaded onto the buses and were taken to the hotel "closest to the airport," as we were told, in fact a forty-five-minute drive. But we did not care; we did not have a performance that evening; we were resting.

The next day, we calmly, without haste, arrived at the airport, flew to Moscow, and finally were reunited with our families.

But it turned out that the rest period is not so restful for us. In four days (only four days!) we are scheduled to leave Moscow for Czechoslovakia for a month-long tour.

We were all exhausted both physically and emotionally. As for me, I slept for almost two days—forty hours without a break. According to conversations I had with fellow dancers, everyone had similar experiences. Our bodies demanded rest.

The management of the ensemble, knowing that we were in good shape but physically exhausted, canceled rehearsals and gave us the opportunity to relax with our families and gather strength. But we called each other and kept in touch with the leadership of the ensemble so we would not miss receiving instructions for departure. And for good reason.

WHERE ARE THE COSTUMES?

Two days before departure, it turned out that we, the artists, were ready, but many of our costumes had not arrived from South America. Well, some of them arrived. The dresses for the round dance and the men's costumes had arrived, but there were no shoes, hats, or accessories for any of the dances. Dancers without shoes? Impossible! The missing items were neither in Moscow nor Czechoslovakia. They were stuck at some Western European airport.

Fyodor Ivanovich Shestakov, the head of our production department and the technical director of the ensemble, was urgently sent to Holland. He knew by heart how many boxes were to arrive at the concert and what was packed in each of the more than one hundred boxes.

In the meantime, we artists and musicians took the train to Czechoslovakia. In a calm (relatively) atmosphere, in a tight and shaky compartment of the train, some of us began to calculate which dances could go on unchanged because we had costumes, shoes, and accessories for them and which dances would need to be changed and how we would change them. Some dances might have to be removed from the program entirely.

It was good that, on this tour, we were not scheduled to start our performances in the capital of the country or from any major city. The first performances would be held in peripheral areas. There would be no major press coverage. We all hoped that the missing costumes would arrive from Europe, but our collective nervousness was overwhelming.

PART 3

Around the World
with Russian Dance

CZECHOSLOVAKIA

We arrived for our month in Czechoslovakia on November 19, 1973. We had only some of our costumes and props, and we still were not sure where the rest of our costumes were.

Shoes!

We arrived for the rehearsal early, but no one knows exactly what parts of our performance we will be able to do. It all depends on whether our costumes arrive. Just in case they will arrive, we decided to do a full rehearsal.

Suddenly, however, we receive another surprise! But this time it is a pleasant one. Only forty minutes before the performance, a worker brings a large bag of shoes—men's and women's—and dump them out onto the center of the stage. Where did these come from? It turned out that the local amateur dance ensemble had been able to offer some friendly help when they learned of our predicament! We interrupted the rehearsal and pounced on this pile of shoes, trying to pair up the shoes and find ones that fit us. The Czechs use the same boots and shoes for their dances as we Russians do. What a nice coincidence! It was a difficult scramble, but we are finally able to start the performance. We can dance!

First Performance

In our dance "Siberian Suite," we have our bear suit and the pitchforks for hunting the bear, but we have no men's fur hats! Well, we will dance without our hats. Let the Czechs think that Siberian hunters are so strong they can walk around Siberia in winter without hats. In reality, of course, it is impossible to spend fifteen minutes without a hat in the cold. But we have to dance contrary to the truth of life because our hats had not arrived. It was okay. Our brave hunters danced in the Siberian frost without hats.

From the very beginning of the performance, we felt that the reaction of the Czech audience to our dances was exactly the same as that of the Russians. They also freeze and hold their breath during the amazing and unique Nadezhdina's round dances, just as the Russians do. They wildly applaude the men's tricks and acrobatic jumps. In general, we felt at home, in a familiar environment. This helped to release the tension a little that we had been feeling over the loss of our costumes.

At the end of the concert, as we were getting ready for the big Cossack Dance, I see my friend, the soloist-jumper Zhenya Kudryavtsev, wrapping a thick terrycloth towel around his leg. "What are you doing?" I ask him.

"My borrowed boots are two sizes too big! I hope this keeps them from flying off when I jump!"

And so, in boots in the style of "Chaplin's boots," he goes on stage to dance the gallant Cossack dance. I wait nervously for his solo. Zhenya should jump a whole circle of sixteen jumps, raising both legs to his head each time. This jump is called *pike in the turn*. It is one of the most difficult jumps, and only few dancers in the entire Soviet Union can do it. And so Zhenya is jumping his pike. I watch closely to see what will happen. The first jump, the second … It is going well. Now the seventh, the eighth … On his fifteenth jump, Zhenya's right boot flies off into the wings. He jumps the sixteenth jump on inertia alone wearing only one boot. But he does it perfectly and elegantly without one boot in time to the music. He lands on one knee as if nothing had happened.

The audience, obviously realizing our difficulties and seeing how we worked through difficult situations with honor, applauds us wildly! For us, such an outstanding reception is really a reward for this uncommonly difficult concert. We had all been so very nervous. The next day we were scheduled to move to the next city; we would at least be able to relax emotionally.

Our Travels through Czechoslovakia

We travel through Czechoslovakia on buses at a leisurely pace. Most of our routes are along narrow rural roads. We make our way slowly, and fatigue builds up, but we can see the local life up close. Sometimes we stop and can drink some fine Czech beer like ordinary locals. Usually on our travel days we do not have a performance, so we do not risk anything by having a beer or two; it would not affect the quality of the next performance.

One day, we arrive in a new city where we will be performing. When we arrive at the theater, we find out that the director of our production department, Fyodor Ivanovich Shestakov, caught up with us. He had finally secured our theatrical baggage and brought it from Holland! We all heaved great sighs of relief. All the shoes, all the hats, all the dance accessories—everything is here with us. We can work confidently without hassle.

In a free minute before the start of the concert, a crowd of artists surrounded Fyodor Ivanovich. Everyone is interested in how he, who does not know a single language of the world except for Russian, found a pilot in a foreign airline and made an agreement with him. Fyodor Ivanovich's story was short. He was a man of few words. "Well, they showed me his plane. I asked which hotel. It turned out to be the same hotel where I was staying. I went to his room in the evening and put a bottle of vodka on the table. In general, we agreed." The famous comedian writer Zhvanetsky later described this situation with the participation of vodka more accurately: "You don't understand me. I don't understand you. But together we understand each other."

So, we continued our journey across Czechoslovakia from city to city. Czechoslovakia is a very beautiful country—mountains and forests and nature in general were all pleasing to the eye. But the cities were like one other. Maybe this was an example of Big Brother— the Soviet Union played a role?

Three cities were strikingly different from other cities—Prague, the capital of the Czech Republic; Bratislava, the capital of Slovakia; and Brno, the capital of Moravia. The unique historical architecture of Prague, the soft green landscapes of Bratislava and the industrial character of Brno—everything was unusual and interesting.

And as we drove along the empty fields of Czechoslovakia, we saw four-meter-high poles, which we learned were supports for hops. This was the foundation to produce the world-famous Czech beer. These poles were familiar to me from the sensational musical film *Love in Hop*, which made a splash in Moscow, with the famous singer Karel Gott in the title role.

Our performances continued. In every city, there were over-crowded halls and invariably warm receptions from audiences. As I mentioned earlier, the reaction of the Czechoslovak audiences was exactly the same as the reaction of our Soviet audiences. We felt at home during our time in Czechoslovakia. In general, Czechs (we used one common word to call both Czechs and Slovaks throughout the country) are a very open, honest, and friendly people. We were often invited to people's homes after performances for dinner and to spend the evening; restaurants were not held in high esteem. Many people spoke Russian with an accent, but we understood them. Sometimes, for dinner and conversation, we stayed up so late that our hosts could not take us back to our hotel, so we were left us to spend the night in their homes. The atmosphere in the entire country and the people's attitude toward us was so friendly. We could behave almost as if we were at home with relatives.

On the "Crystal Plane" to Moscow

With frequent performances and almost daily slow travel, we did not have the opportunity to wander around the cities and see anything new. There was no time even to run to a nearby store and buy something. Unspent money burned in our pockets.

And then, the day we were to depart Czechoslovakia arrived. At the airport, we unexpectedly—another pleasant surprise—saw a small shop full of magnificent, first-class-quality Czech crystal. We knocked the only saleswoman off her feet! She tried very hard and still did not have time to fulfill the requests of a large group of artists whom she had seen on stage just the day before!

"Do you want this vase or that?"

"Both! And one more also!"

Hurriedly wrapping our purchases (the plane would not wait), the saleswoman gave us a rare, one might say, double compliment: "You buy as quickly and easily as you dance!"

On this pleasant note, we plunged into what became known as the "crystal plane" and flew to Moscow to be reunited with our families and enjoy the New Year celebration.

Happy to Be Home

In four months, in South America and Czechoslovakia, we had experienced a military coup, presidential elections with a murder, a stage breaking under our feet, dangerous cities full of thieves and kidnappers, travels on buses and flights on planes, then planes again (endless planes), meetings with interesting people, and performances at transcendental heights. Yes, the performances continued invariably, in any and all conditions, because performing was our main job. In four months, we gave more than seventy performances! We were happy that we had withstood such a load and were now returning home to our families.

We did not yet know what adventures awaited us next!

Beryozka. 'Spinning Wheel' Round Dance

Eugene Kudryavtsev

Kudryavtsev. Cossack Dance. The Pike Jump

SPAIN

The new year, 1974, began. For us, the artists of the Beryozka State Choreographic Ensemble, life went on as usual with rehearsals, staging new dances, and giving performances. My daughter, Natasha, was one year old in February. As a result of her dad's four-month trip to South America and Czechoslovakia, she no longer recognized me and was initially afraid. She cried at my approach and hid behind her mommy. But I made friends with her again. We played and walked together, enjoying communication.

Soon, however, the ensemble's upcoming plans were announced. We were going to Spain. We received this message with calm satisfaction. We had already been to Spain three years previously in 1971. Performing for two months, we had traveled all over the country. We visited big cities and in small ones. We saw resorts on the shores of the Mediterranean Sea and in the Basquiat mountains. We had seen performances of the best bullfighters such as El Córdobes and Manuel Ortiz, and we had seen performances of the best flamenco dancers—Antonio Soler, Antonio Gades, and Maruja Garrido—and had also talked with them. It seemed that nothing could surprise us. Therefore, we took the news of the trip to Spain rather calmly.

But this time, Spain surprised us with weather and nature. Having taken off at the end of February from snowy, blizzard Moscow, we found ourselves in a warm, but not hot, sunny Spain. We could go to the beach. The water was still cold, and bathing was out of the question, but in those cities that were by the sea, we basked and gained solar energy.

Nothing had changed in the cities themselves. The stores sold the same items they had sold when we were there before, and at the same prices. Locals instantly lined up to purchase goods at cheap prices. Under Generalissimo Franco, the country had not changed, and people did not live well.

In the middle of our month-long tour of Spain, details of our continued trip to France began to emerge. More precisely, we were going to Paris to open the new Palais des Congrès. We were going to be the very first performers on the stage of the most prestigious building in France! What an honor! We were so excited!

It seemed odd that such an international city as Paris—one might say a crossroads of world roads—did not have a facility equal to the Kremlin Palace of Congresses in Moscow, which was opened back in 1961 and is now known as the Kremlin Palace of Congresses. And now, in 1974, the French government had asked the Soviet government to send particularly the Beryozka Dance Company to open their main palace of the country.

Having successfully finished our concerts in several small cities of Spain, we boarded a plane for a short flight to Paris.

Spain, Madrid. Nadejdina, Soler. Bow

Spain, Madrid. Russian Waltz 'Birch'. Koltsova

Spain, Madrid. Cossack Dance. Shagalov

Spain. Famous Dancer Antonio Soler

Spain. Flamenco Dancer Maruja Garrido

Spain. Flamenco Dancer Maruja Garrido

Spain. Flamenco Dancer Antonio Gades

Spain. Bullfighter Manuel Ortiz

Spain. Bullfighter El Cordobez

Spain, Madrid

Spain, Madrid. Prado Museum

Spain, Barcelona

PARIS

*T*he day after we landed in Paris, we boarded large, comfortable buses and were solemnly and slowly driven to the huge new building known as the Palais des Congrès.

The solemnity of the situation was that the French government had asked the Soviet dance ensemble (honorary foreigners!) to open the country's most prestigious stage—concert hall number one—which was the Palais des Congrès in Paris. And the Soviet government had agreed.

But it was not enough to open the new venue and be the first to perform on a new stage, which was an honor in itself. The French government had offered us the opportunity to give forty-five performances on that stage! They were so confident in our success that they planned for such a long engagement!

As I think back on the tours of various collectives, either Soviet in foreign countries or foreigners in the Soviet Union—dance, drama, or orchestral companies—I cannot find anything analogues to our performances in Paris. It was a unique case!

For comparison, I remembered the famous New York City Ballet tour under the direction of the outstanding choreographer George Balanchine in 1962 in Moscow. I was a young, aspiring artist and tried to gain experience by watching all the ballet and dance groups touring in the USSR, so I remembered those tours. And this tour was famous because it took place at the state level under the patronage of the United States State Department and the USSR Ministry of Foreign Affairs. The entire ballet world of Moscow was extraordinarily excited. Tickets were sold out instantly and resold for huge sums of money. The names of the hitherto unknown Jacques D'Amboise and Edward Villella were remembered forever, and all Moscow male dancers tried to repeat their unprecedented jumps during rehearsals the day after the performance.

Simultaneously with the New York City Ballet's tour in the USSR, the Bolshoi Theater's ballet tour took place in the United States. Both teams tried their best. Through these tours, the governments of each country wanted to prove the superiority not only of its ballet, but of its social systems as a whole!

So, the duration of the performances of the American ballet in Moscow was five weeks, and the Americans performed on two stages: the Kremlin Palace of Congresses and the Bolshoi Theater. But the performances of Beryozka in 1974 in Paris went on for six weeks! And on the same stage, and it is much more difficult to maintain the interest of the audience for such a long time in one place. So, the uniqueness of the performances of Beryozka in Paris remained unsurpassed!

Inside Palais des Congrès

When we arrived, the inside the building was a mess. There were many workers on the stage hanging the wings and sweeping up the construction waste. In the artists' dressing rooms, female builders were washing tables, chairs, and floors in preparation for the famous artists—us!

We sat in the front rows of the hall waiting for the stage to be ready for our rehearsal. As we waited, we discussed the rules of conduct in the new Palace, and we discussed the schedule for the next six weeks in Paris. Meanwhile, the stage was still not ready.

Next to us, a meeting of the ticket attendants of the new building was taking place. They were mostly young French women, and they looked at us with interest. Well, of course, famous Russian dancers would be performing in their new building for a month and a half! It was so unusual! But the woman who was their manager did not interrupt her speech; she did not allow them to be distracted by us for a long time.

We finally ran out to topics to discuss, but the stage was still not ready. Our management decided to change our schedule for the day. While the workers were finishing cleaning the stage, we were released into the city for two hours. Everyone quickly and habitually gathered into small groups and set out into the city to see and study Paris. I decided differently. We would be in Paris for forty-five days; the city would be there for the entire time. I decided to stay and wander around the building. It was interesting to compare this building with our Kremlin Palace of Congresses, which I know very well inside.

I went out into an empty foyer and went, as they say, wherever my eyes were looking. A passing man stopped and asked if he could help me with something. I explained that I was an artist of the Beryozka Dance Company, and we had just arrived for the first time in a new building. The man was glad to meet a Russian artist and, without expressing surprise at my French, suggested, "Do you want me to show you the whole building?" Of course, I gladly agreed. It turned out that this man was the chief engineer of the Palais de Congrès. I could not have imagined a better guide!

First, we went to the lower floors under the auditorium where we saw rooms for meetings and discussions. Now I realized that the main function of the Palais des Congrès was not concerts, not entertainment. The Palais des Congrès had been created for congresses and large gatherings. There were forty-six meeting rooms! Moreover, in each of the rooms, in the middle of the side wall, there was a hidden accordion-style, soundproof hidden wall that could be pulled out to turn one large room into two smaller ones. Thus, ninety-two rooms for small groups could be easily created.

We went up to the level of the auditorium. There were actually two auditoriums. We will perform in the large one, which held 3,400 seats. (Later it was increased to 3,700 seats.) The smaller auditorium held 650 seats. On this floor, I could see the similarities between the Palais des Congrès and the Palace of Congresses in Moscow. Both palaces are "sunk" into the ground so that most of both buildings lies below street level. The governments of both countries—the USSR and France—did not want these huge buildings to dominate the general architectural flavor of their respective cities, Moscow and Paris. But the Kremlin Palace of Congresses can accommodate 6,000 spectators—almost twice the capacity of the Paris facility!

As we rose higher into the building, the chief engineer took me to the "holy of holies"—to his radio and television studio. From here, he himself directs the progress of the performance including changes in sound and light. He proudly shows me his sophisticated audio equipment including large tape recorders. This studio is completely professional and able to broadcast concerts or meetings all over the country! The chief engineer then shows me a highlight of the studio—video cameras with which he can observe everything that happens not only on the stage, but most importantly, throughout the auditorium! "Look at the screen," he tells me, and he turns a few buttons. This activates the small, almost-invisible cameras installed on the walls of the main hall. We examine the entire hall, and then he zooms in for a closeup of two chairs—two of 3,400 spectator seats! At this time, the hall is empty, but I can easily imagine observing someone suspicious in the auditorium. People in this control room can clearly see what anyone in the audience is doing. This is security! This is control!

Opening the Palace of Congrès: First Performance

Finally, the day of the grand opening of the Palais des Congrès was determined. The French government kindly gave us three days to prepare for our performance—to "settle down" on the stage. All of us—the French government; the company of the best French impresario, Georges Soria, organizing our tours; the French people who work at the Palace; and, of course, we, the artists—want the opening of the main concert stage in France to be held at the highest level!

The opening day. There are three people on the stage: the minister of culture of France; the ambassador of the USSR in France; and the founder of the Beryozka Dance Company, Nadezhda Sergeevna Nadezhdina. The translator is behind the group, translating in a low voice. It was decided not to bring any of the artists on stage until the actual performance begins, until the music of the first round dance (this type of dance is known as *khorovod*) will be played by the orchestra. The music and subsequent appearance of artists in gloriously colored costumes should make a deep impression on the audience and remain in their memory. And it paid off—it worked!

Nadezhda Sergeevna stood in the center of the stage and was silent. She could have said a lot, and I am sure she would have said it in brilliant French, but she was silent. She received the honor and respect of France! As a birthday man receives pleasant words of congratulations addressed to him on his birthday, as a hero of the day receives praises worthy of his merits on his glorious day, she did not need to speak. The worldwide fame of the ensemble, earned over the years, spoke for her.

In a short speech, the minister of culture of France noted the importance of the arrival of our ensemble for all of France, not only for Paris, and not only in the cultural sense, but also in a diplomatic one, raising relations between our countries to a new level. In an even shorter speech, the ambassador of the USSR to France not only confirmed the importance of the arrival of our ensemble to France, but commented on the high artistic level of the ensemble. Then the quiet, calm music of the round dance "Birch" sounded, and the girls began to appear on the stage. The audience burst into applause! With some kind of sixth sense, the girls "heard" the music; in actuality, they could not hear it over the applause. The applause continued almost without interruption during the entire round dance! This was a rare success.

The audience gradually began to calm down during the following numbers, but each solo and each trick caused a new burst of applause. Their enthusiasm cheered us up and added new energy to our performance. We were all extremely excited; the performance continued on an extremely high level! At the end of the program, after the "Great Cossack Dance," the audience stood and applauded for so long, we were unable to leave the stage! We could not calm down for a long time. We were drunk on the overwhelming energy created that evening.

Avenue des Champs-Élysées

The Parisian spring weather was lovely. It was not as warm as it had been in Spain a week previously, but it was sunny, and a light breeze brought fresh air into the city. The central boulevard of Paris, the Champs-Élysées, was full of people who had been longing for warmth and sun. The Palais des Congrès was located on the nearby Place de la Porte Maillot in the vicinity of the famous Place de l'Étoile (Place Charles de Gaulle) as well as the Avenue Champs-Élysées. We often walked along the Champs-Élysées, past luxury shops, art galleries, shopping arcades and countless restaurants.

As the charming and beloved Joe Dassin sang in 1969 in his instantly popular song "Champs-Élysées":

On the Champs-Élysées, on the Champs-Élysées

In the sun, in the rain, at noon or midnight

There is anything you want

On the Champs-Élysées.

In fact, Joe Dassin was called Monsieur Champs-Élysées because of this song!

It was interesting to see that the chairs in all the restaurants along the Champs-Élysées were not set around the tables as usual; rather, they were turned toward the street. All the chairs! This changed the mood. Now dining out was a theater experience. "Spectators," comfortably sitting in restaurants and cafes over meals, cups of coffee, or glasses of wine watched the endless crowd flowing along the street. And the "artists" walking down the street looked at the "spectators" with interest as well. The atmosphere was relaxed. When walking people saw acquaintances sitting at a table, they unceremoniously sat down with them. This was clearly in the order of things. Quick conversations over fresh cups of coffee or glasses of wine immediately began. And the conversation, we noticed, was fast. No one in France, in any city, speaks faster than Parisians. The waiters worked very quickly. The action of the "street theater" did not stop for a second.

Soon, our daily schedule of performances began. We played seven performances every week. On Saturday, there were two performances, the matinée and the evening, and on Sunday, there was only one daytime, and the evening was free. We took advantage of our free Sunday evenings to watch French concerts and entertainment, of which there are countless numbers in Paris.

Zizi Jeanmaire and Roland Petit

So, at the invitation of our impresario, Monsieur Soria, we attended the famous Moulin Rouge (Red Mill) cabaret. Everything was unusual for us in this performance. Various genres combined in one concert reminded us of pop concerts in Moscow, but the action went on continuously without introductions to the different numbers and without stopping. First, we were treated to the famous French cancan performed by topless dancers (topless!). The action quickly switched to acrobatics, and from there to several humorous numbers. Suddenly, however, we hold our breath—it was a solo classical ballet performance by a mesmerizing ballerina, the petite Zizi Jeanmaire, who unexpectedly took us into the pure world of classical dance. As we later learned, Zizi Jeanmair was the star of the French classical stage, the star of all of France, who appeared in several films that revolved around classical ballet. She danced with such stars as Rudolf Nureyev and Mikhail Baryshnikov!

She was also the wife of the famous choreographer Roland Petit, and the story of their lives together is amazing. They first met at ballet school when they were nine years old, and since that time, they have not parted.

Together they studied dancing at the Grand Opera Ballet School in Paris, one of the best ballet schools in the world. Roland began his stage work early, excelling as a choreographer. And he began to stage dance numbers for his Zizi, whose capabilities he knew better than anyone else.

They gained real world fame: Roland as a stage director, Zizi as a ballerina. In 1949, Roland staged the ballet and film-ballet *Carmen* in London. Of course, his beloved Zizi played the role of Carmen, and he played the role of jealous, loving Jose. The ballet was performed on the stages of different countries, and a film version played around the world, bringing even more popularity to Roland and Zizi.

They got married when they turned 30 in 1954, and they lived together for fifty-seven years! In 2011, Roland passed away at eighty-seven years old. Zizi survived her beloved by nine years and passed away in 2020 at the age of ninety-six.

Roland and Zizi's creative lives were unusually active and full. Zizi was incredibly talented! In her ballet career, Carmen became her title role and calling card. Zizi performed this ballet on Broadway for several seasons in different years. She traveled the world with *Carmen*. She danced this role for more than thirty years, which surpasses all ballet records for leading soloists. In 1980, she danced *Carmen* in partnership with Mikhail Baryshnikov! At the time, she was fifty-six years old, which also surpasses all stage longevity records of ballet dancers in leading roles.

In addition to the ballet scene, she was a serious actress, starring in six Hollywood films and she even sang! In 1950 in London, she performed her first song in the show, and her song won a Grand Prix du disque, a prestigious prize in France. And not only she sang, others sang about her too. Charming young singer and composer Peter Sarstedt, in his song "Where Do You Go to My Lovely?" compared Zizi Jeanmaire with the standard of dance. The modern press called Zizi Jeanmaire a superstar and emphasized that she had built a bridge between classical dance and variety shows, combining such different arts. We were lucky to see such an extraordinary artist in the very first days of our stay in Paris!

Roland Petit was also an unusually talented person, and we found it amazing that such a couple had got together. For any choreographer, the creation of a theater, a ballet collective is a great achievement and merit. It is an achievement of a lifetime. But Roland Petit created four ballet theaters; his first being the Ballets des Champs-Élysées when he was only twenty-one years old! This is courage, this is assertiveness!

Roland created his second group, Ballets de Paris, at the age of twenty-four, and, of course, his beloved Zizi was the star of this group. In 1972, when he was forty-eight years old, he founded his last theater, the Ballet National de Marseille, and worked there for twenty-six years.

Roland was invited to stage large and small ballets at the Paris Grand Opera as well as in theaters in Italy, Germany, Great Britain, Canada, and even Cuba. His most famous ballets *were Le Jeune Homme et la Mort* (*The Youth and Death*) (1946), *Carmen* (1949), and *Notre-Dame de Paris* (1965), which the Grand Opera ballet company brought to Moscow. The most famous masters of world choreography worked with Roland Petit. Azari Plisetsky (Maya Plisetskaya's younger brother) worked with him for several years as a teacher-tutor. Rudolf Nureyev wanted to dance *Le Jeune Homme et la Mort*. Maya Plisetskaya gave him ideas, and Roland created two choreographic numbers for her.

In total, Roland Petit created 176 ballets in his life, of which sixty were for his always beloved Zizi Jeanmaire. I do not know of a single choreographer in the world who is close in performance to Roland Petit.

After the intermission at the Moulin Rouge, the program continued. And it ended, of course, with an eternally young, temperamental French cancan performed by topless dancers! Our impressions of this experience overwhelmed us!

Back to Champs-Élysées

The Parisians, especially those who worked in the Champs-Élysées region, were aware of our performances. Wherever we went—art galleries, chic stores, or music centers—Parisians, hearing our accent, would ask the inevitable question: "Are you from Beryozka?" Many had already bought tickets, while others asked us in detail about the schedule of performances with the clear intention of going buying tickets to see us.

The owner of a chic women's clothing store, flattered by our visit to his store and extremely delighted with an interesting conversation with Russian celebrities (I fluently translated from Russian into French and vice versa), promised that, in exactly two days, he would be sitting in the front row. Indeed, two days later, on Wednesday, he was sitting in the front row dressed in chic white pants, black jacket, and bright tie. In a jaunty American way, he threw one leg over his opposite knee, smiled broadly at us, and obviously wanted to show with every one of his actions that he was "our man" in Beryozka.

The day after the concert, we were walking along the Champs-Élysées, and entered his store. He was twice delighted: from our performance, and from the fact that he could easily talk to such world-famous performers. And after another two days he came to another performance! And again, he was sitting in the first row dressed in his chic clothing, sitting in that defiant American way with legs crossed, and smiling broadly at us.

French Music

When we first entered our hotel room, I noticed radio on the nightstands between the beds. I began to investigate this receiver because I knew we would have to live with it for a month and a half. And it turned out that we were in luck! We did not have to listen only to what the hotel offered us; we could search the broadcast stations to find what we were interested in. Immediately, I started manipulating the tuner to find music I liked. After quickly listening to several channels, I found a station that broadcast modern popular French music, mostly songs.

I have loved French music since childhood, from the moment we started learning French in the first grade of the Bolshoi Theater Choreographic Academy when I was but ten years old. It became interesting to me to learn the music of the people who speak such a beautiful language. And the French songs did not disappoint my expectations.

Directly opposite our school, at the corner of Pushechnaya Street and Neglinka, there was a music store with a department that sold gramophone records. I began to go there sometimes and browse through the records.

When Edith Piaf's records began to be sold in the Soviet Union, I managed to buy almost all of them. I listened to them hundreds of times, memorizing the music and trying to translate and understand the words of the songs. I was very interested in the meanings of the songs.

Then came the recordings of Yves Montand. There were not that many released in the Soviet Union, but I knew he was a modern singer, and I tried to buy a lot of his records. It was easy to understand him and translate. Since Yves Montand, besides being a singer, was also a drama theater and film actor, he had very clear pronunciation. And I admired the soul he put into his famous songs about Paris—"*A Paris*" ("In Paris"), "*J'aime flâner sur les grands boulevards*" ("I love to walk along the Grand Boulevards"), and "*Les feuilles mortes*" ("Fallen leaves").

On my radio in my Paris hotel room, I found a wave of the most modern French songs. There I stopped. Why do I love French music and especially songs? Melody is the basis of French songs, and so many of the melodies are close to those of Russian songs. Yes, the melodies of Russian and French songs are different; after all, the melody of Russian songs is firmly connected with Russian colloquial speech. Still, the basis of the French song is the melody, not the rhythm, as is often the case in the English-speaking countries.

French songs are not only well and competently written, they are diverse—more varied than, say, Italian or Spanish songs. So many of them are poems and ballads about love. Some are reflections on life or childhood memories that touch the heart of any person. Some are tragedies. And the French put heartfelt lyrical poetry into these songs!

The biggest tragedy of life is the collapse of love. For example, the song of the singer Nicoletta, *"Il est mort le soleil"* ("It died—the sun"). She begins it with a high note and almost screaming:

It is dead!

It is dead—the sun!

When you left me.

It is dead—summer.

Love and the sun are alike.

And here is an example that has become a classic—an example of happy love: Edith Piaf's *"La Vie en Rose"* ("Life in a Rosy Light"):

When he takes me in his arms

He whispers to me

I see life in a rosy light.

He speaks words of love to me

Words of every day

And it does something to me.

And here is another variation on the theme of love, or rather, an affair at the ball. The famous singer Salvatore Adamo, in the song *"Vous permettez, monsieur?"* ("Will you allow me, monsieur") (1964), plays an entire performance in one song:

Will you allow me, monsieur,

engager your daughter?

(And although he smiles at me,

I see he doesn't trust)

Will you allow me, monsieur?

We promise to be wiser

How were you in our years

Right up to the wedding night.

The audience loved this song. They loved it so much that, if Salvatore did not include it into the program, the entire audience would sing it to him, and Salvatore would stand in the center of the stage smiling modestly.

One of the most famous love songs was incredibly popular worldwide. In the original, in French, it is called *"Les feulles mortes"* ("Dead Leaves"). It was composed in 1945 by Joseph Kosma, and the lyrics were written by Jacques Prévert. In Russian, it was translated more literally as "Fallen Leaves." In English, the song is called "Autumn Leaves." First time performed back in 1946, it has been translated into many languages and sung by countless singers. It continues to be one of the most popular songs in the world.

One of the most classic renditions of this song was by Yves Montand, the first person to record the song. Montand, a wonderful actor, immersed viewers and listeners in memories as he performed this romantic song slowly, as if pondering over every word and emotion:

This song reminds me of us

You, you loved me and I, I loved you

We both lived together

You who loved me, I who loved you

But life divides those who love

Very slow, no noise

And the sea washes away on the sand

Traces of separated lovers.

A Day in the Life of an Artist

How was the day of the ensemble artist on tour organized? We were in Paris for a long time and worked on the same stage for seven weeks. With such an unusual sedentary life, we developed a special daily regimen.

We began our mornings with some quick gymnastic exercises. We could not start the day without this; otherwise, our muscles and joints would ache all day. After an even quicker breakfast—"To the city!" With this short phrase, we named several hours of our long walks through different districts of Paris. Sometimes we took guided bus tours and visited museums and, of course, shops. At home in the Soviet Union, during our tours, we saw interesting cities, museums, and theaters. But there were no shops; rather, there were no shops like the ones we visited in other parts of the world, especially Paris. There was a severely small choice of goods offered for sale in Russian shops; in fact, the goods on the shelves both in Ivanovo and in Vladivostok (or name any other city of your choice) were the same.

When we were abroad, however, we couldn't find two identical stores! All the trading companies took pride in their inventory and flaunted the very best they had. This forced competition, which was good for the shoppers. Each store offered a completely different variety of goods, and all the best that a company could be proud of was on display. Undoubtedly, we tried to seize the opportunity to find and bring home what we could not find in the Soviet

Union—clothes, shoes, children's toys, music (new recordings), and sometimes books.

Since our hotel was located on the outskirts of the city center, we usually used two methods of transport to the center of Paris—a bus to the La Defense Paris Métro station, then a Métro train. One of the oldest rapid transit systems in the world, the Paris Métro connected old lines (slow, small carriages) and new lines (modern, fast, and comfortable cars). Of course, it was interesting for us to ride on the old cars where we could experience the "smell" and the mood of the past. We didn't have this opportunity at home because Moscow rapid transit cars were both more modern and faster. But the old Métro lines were only in the city center of Paris.

Our time for walking around the city was limited. The ensemble was governed by the strictest discipline. We had to be back at the hotel at two o'clock in the afternoon. This was our favorite time for listening to music on the Paris radio. While we were preparing lunch, and then during the lunch, we enjoyed beautiful tunes, absorbed the French mood, and became, at least for a short time, residents of Paris.

This was followed by the obligatory one and a half to two hours of sleep. It was an order because it was necessary to accumulate strength for the concert. Only after such a rest could we perform each concert with full dedication and explosive energy! This order had been developed decades earlier, and it justified itself by the quality of the dance.

After each concert, returning to the hotel, relaxed and relieved from the stress of work, we would again turn on the radio station we loved and immerse ourselves in French music at dinner and, as it were, we became Parisians.

Popular Music on Paris Radio: Gilbert Becaud and Jacques Brel

Thus, having chosen several stations that broadcast popular music, we listened to French music in those rare moments of free time when we were at the hotel.

Who was most popular then on the Paris radio waves? The most frequent singers—one might say the hosts of the broadcast—were Gilbert Becaud and Jacques Brel.

Gilbert Bécaud was nicknamed "Monsieur 100,000 Volts" because of his irrepressible energy during his concerts. His career spanned over fifty years, and for many seasons he performed at the Olympia, the best concert hall in Paris. His most popular song was "And Now," written in 1961, repeating the musical pattern of Ravel's "Bolero." But my favorite song was "Nathalie," about his trip to Moscow and his Moscow guide, whose name was Nathalie. This song reminded me of my fifteen-month-old daughter, Natalia, who remained in Moscow with her mother.

Jacques Brel, although he was a Belgian singer, was loved by the French public. He was not only a singer, but also a songwriter, actor, and director who composed and performed his own songs. His songs were special—thoughtful and theatrical. French people like to think about the text of a song. His songs gathered a large number of fans, first in Belgium and France, and then around the world. Jacques Brel was considered a master of modern *chanson*.

To advance to the big stage, at the age of twenty-four, he left Brussels in Belgium, left (temporarily) his family, which had just grown with the birth of a second daughter and, against the desires of his family, moved to Paris. The singer's career was not easy. Jacques accepted any invitations to perform. He sang a lot for Catholic associations, for which he received the nickname Abbot Brel.

Jacques signed up for international tours and traveled to many countries over the years. And although his family moved to Paris to be with him, and he already had three children (all girls), he was constantly on the road. France, Holland, Switzerland, his native Belgium, North Africa, Egypt, USA, Canada, and the Soviet Union. The continuous tour schedule and routes were unpredictable.

But this hard work gradually began to bear fruit. Jacques Brel received international recognition and popularity. Year after year, carving out time, he recorded six albums. He began to receive invitations to perform in prestigious venues, including the Olympia in Paris. He became a partner with such celebrities as Charles Aznavour, Serge Gainsborough, and Zizi Jeanmaire. The press and critics wrote about him with increasing enthusiasm. In 1961, at the age of thirty-two, Jacques Brel was declared the star of the French song! His talent as a dramatic actor was revealed. At his concerts, the audience first cried with grief and then jumped up from their seats and burst into unexpected applause. Critics wrote that his songs were like the seasons when the audience moves from love to passion, to despair, to grief.

Jacques Brel's most famous song was "*Ne me quitte pas*" ("Don't Leave Me"). Critics and audiences have called this song "the most ingenious love song ever." Following Jacques, all the famous singers of France sang this song.

Shortly after his triumphant second tour to the Soviet Union in 1965, Jacques Brel announced his decision to leave the stage. And, despite the requests of colleagues and the public, he did not change his mind. The years 1966 and 1967 passed with farewell concerts around the world.

In 1974, when we danced in Paris, Jacques Brel was no longer singing on stage. But his popularity was still off the charts! His records sold in the millions. He appeared in the musical *The Man from La Mancha* in the title role, Don Quixote. He starred in a total of eleven films. His music was broadcast on French radio and television; he became an everyday singer for the French public and for us as well.

Four years after our time in Paris, in 1978, Jacques Brel passed away at the age of forty-nine in Paris from lung cancer, the result of years of smoking. But he was buried in his beloved Marquesas Islands where he had lived the last years of his life and about which he wrote his last songs. By a strange coincidence, his grave was a few yards away from the grave of another famous Frenchman, painter Paul Gauguin.

Classics French Singers: Yves Montand, Edith Piaf, Charles Aznavour, and Serge Gainsborough

The recognized classics of French singers were Yves Montand, Edith Piaf, and Charles Aznavour; they were often heard on the radio.

Yves Montand really was the soul of the French people. His songs also coincided with the rhythm of the soul of a poet-dreamer who loves Paris:

Under the sky of Paris, a song flies

It was born today in the heart of a boy

Under the sky of Paris, lovers walk

Their happiness rests on a melody composed for them.

Thy also coincided with the feelings of the driver of a heavy truck:

The road is spinning like a long ribbon

Far from cities, far from cities.

If you want to live long

Be attentive to the steering wheel.

Edith Piaf, by the time we were in Paris, had already passed away, but she remained the recognized national singer of France. The French public did not want to recognize anyone as equal to Edith Piaf. And even Mireille Mathieu, who resembled Edith Piaf in voice, repertoire, and even manners, remained in the category of "budding hope" for the discerning French public. Therefore, on the radio we heard Piaf more often than Mathieu.

Charles Aznavour's songs—"*La Bohème*," "*Les Comedians*," "*Emmenez-moi*," "*Et pourtant*"—were already well known to me, and I listened to them with pleasure on the Paris radio. But each time, from the depths of my memory, came my personal recollection of meeting him once upon a time in my youth, in Moscow. Charles Aznavour, although he was famous all over the world, was almost unknown in the Soviet Union. His first album in the Soviet Union was released in small circulation in 1971, much later than the recordings of Edith Piaf and Yves Montand. But, having arrived in the Soviet Union in 1963, Charles Aznavour unexpectedly performed in overcrowded halls and received a warm reception from the public.

It was determined that Charles Aznavour would perform at the Tchaikovsky Concert Hall in Moscow. It was the best concert hall in Moscow. Constructed in the form of a Greek amphitheater, this hall gave each of the 1,500 spectators an excellent view of the performance. The best, most educated, and cultured public in Moscow attended events in this hall.

I knew the Tchaikovsky Concert Hall by heart, inside and out, backstage and in the spectator section. From an early age, even before entering the Bolshoi Ballet School, I performed on this stage as part of the Pioneer Ensemble. And later, as a student of the Ballet Academy, I attended classes at the Tchaikovsky Concert Hall, and we had rehearsals and gave performances on this famous stage.

Of course, as a person who studied French and loved French music, I really wanted to see Charles Aznavour. I knew his name, but I did not know his songs. But how could I see his performance? There was no hope that I could buy a ticket.

As soon as a poster announcing Charles Aznavour's performance appeared on the wall of the Tchaikovsky Concert Hall, an exciting thought occurred to me—why not try to apply my knowledge of the Tchaikovsky Concert Hall to get into Charles Aznavour's concert?

I could not tell anyone about this. But on the day of the concert, I came in advance at the service entrance of the Tchaikovsky Hall. The security service did not pay attention to me; I looked like all student dancers who studied at the Hall. I went to the backstage area. For a long time, I wandered through different rooms and studios, and before the beginning of the concert, I went to the audience area. Members of the audience were already walking into the foyer. Again, no one paid attention to me.

When the ushers opened the doors and let the audience into the hall, I went into the hall, but I knew there would be no free seats. Only at the last minute did I sit down on a step near the stage.

And almost immediately, Charles Aznavour came onto the stage and began to sing. There was no special flamboyant announcement, no introduction of the great actor. Only song after song. And Charles Aznavour's songs were unusual for the Soviet audience. They were without pathos, without posture, in the manner of talking with the viewer or telling the viewer about something personal, intimate.

That day I heard Aznavour's songs for the first time. And, despite the fact that it was a new, unusual style of singing, and I had listened to songs that I had not heard before, I noticed for myself and remembered some of them: "*La Boheme*," "*Mama*," "*Ave Maria*," "*Et pourtant*" ("And yet"). These songs I remembered immediately!

And suddenly, I heard the familiar tune, although it had never been performed before either on stage or on the radio: "Romance (for Two Guitars")! This gypsy song was considered in our country a song from a series of "thieves"—vulgar ones. It was sung in drinking gatherings and at parties, but never on stage. And now, suddenly, a world-famous singer on the stage of the famous Tchaikovsky Concert Hall was singing it! He even sang a refrain in Russian: "Oh, one more time, many more, many times ..." Yes, there was no doubt, Charles Aznavour sang a Russian song! At the end of the song, he picked up the pace and went on a rampage, almost dancing. Of course, our audience accepted "Two Guitars" with a bang!

For me, the concert flew by in an instant. The audience was dumbfounded by his style, which was unusual to a Soviet audience. They applauded continuously; no one wanted to leave the hall. But, sadly enough, I had to go home. I did not want to mix with the crowd of unfamiliar spectators, and I decided to leave the Tchaikovsky Concert Hall in the same way I had entered—through the service entrance backstage.

As I walked across the stage to the exit, I noticed that the door to the artist's dressing room was open. It was a small room, and it was the closest to the stage, so only the most eminent actors prepared for their performances there. I heard voices speaking French. Curiosity got the better of me, and I looked in. Charles Aznavour and several of his assistants were in the room. They noticed me at the door. It would have been extremely impolite of me to leave without saying anything, so I went into the room and went straight to Charles Aznavour. Everyone fell silent as they watched me. Using my French, which, at that time, was quite poor, I expressed my gratitude to Charles Aznavour for the concert and added that his performance was wonderful— marvelous! I was an eighteen-year-old aspiring artist, and I simply did not know what people said to great artists after a triumphant performance. I could not express my feelings.

But Charles Aznavour understood me. He autographed two of his photographs and handed them to me. Then he added two colored ballpoint pens to the photographs (there were no such pens in the Soviet Union yet). His, Charles Aznavour's, name was embossed on the pens. He said goodbye to me with a slight nod of his head. He looked somewhat confused. Charles Aznavour apparently expected many viewers to come to thank him and say warm words after such a success. But I was alone!

The reason for such strange behavior, for the Western world at least, I think, was the disunity of the Soviet Union from the rest of the world. Yes, Soviet people were afraid to communicate with foreigners, especially those from capitalist countries. They were afraid of being accused of worshiping the Western lifestyle, a practice that could stain a lifetime. Yes, I could not show to anyone except my parents these souvenirs, which had been presented to me by Charles Aznavour himself. The gift would inevitably raise unpleasant questions. But the memory of this short meeting and my love of Charles Aznavour's songs lives with me forever.

Among the singers of the older generation, there was one singer whose songs were performed less often, but his songs were very memorable and caused much excitement. Lucien Ginsburg was the son of Jewish immigrants from Russia who fled from the Bolsheviks from Feodosia, Ukraine, during the Civil War and later fled the Nazis from Paris during World War II. When Ginsburg became an adult, he changed his name from Lucien Ginsburg to Serge Gainsborough. The talented young man gravitated toward painting and music. Deciding that he did not have enough talent to become a painter, he continued to make music, accompanying singers in clubs and composing songs for himself, for a future, keeping them, as one says, in the back of his desk drawer.

Having accidentally learned about his talent as a songwriter, his employers forced Serge to go on stage and sing his songs. He started recording albums. He was then invited to work in the cinema, first as a composer, and then as an actor-singer.

To complement his deep male bass voice, Serge Gainsborough chose female partners who had very high, thin, girlish voices. This turned out to be an erotic contrast, and Serge found his "niche"— songs with erotic content in which the girl confessed her love to him and expressed her passion with frequent sexy breathing. His songs quickly gained recognition and popularity in England and France, but not in the Soviet Union where songs of this kind were generally prohibited. I could not believe my ears when I first listened to Serge's songs on the radio. I didn't know that it was possible to transmit such frank feelings broadly—on the radio! His most famous song—his "calling card"—was his 1967 song, "I love you… But I don't anymore…." He composed this song for Brigitte Bardot. This song received highest recognition in England and Ireland but was restricted in several European countries because of its overly sexual content.

Serge Gainsborough drank a lot, smoked mercilessly, boozed all night long, and used foul language. He was not *portraying* a bad boy; he *was* a bad boy. But French audiences believed that man who sang softly and also smoked while he sang was more French than anyone else who could be found in France. He was rude to women, but the women loved him. The entire country knew about his wives and girlfriends. For a long time, Brigitte Bardot was his girlfriend—one of the most beautiful and most famous film actresses in the world. He had met her on the set of a film. Serge's other girlfriend and partner in the songs, Jane Birkin, even after Serge's death in 1991, remained popular and was often invited to appear on television to share her memories of Serge.

After the death of Serge Gainsborough, winner of many song awards, France suddenly felt the loss of a part of its national character.

Youth on Parisian Radio: Mireille Mathieu, Claude François, Gerard Lenorman, and Michel Sardou

Young singers also were heard on the Parisian radio. Among them were bright, memorable singers. But I must say that the French audience is very careful about accepting new, young singers. It has always been. And so it was with all the young singers.

These aspiring stars spent years filled with hard work, rehearsals, searches for their own style, occasional concerts here and there, and endless studio recording sessions, which they had to pay for themselves, counting on future recognition and future success, both popular and financial. Many singers first won recognition in other countries, sometimes in former French colonies, and only then did they return to France. Then the audiences were supportive and changed their attitude toward the singers.

This was exactly what happened to one of the greatest singers of France, Mireille Mathieu. She was born in the south of France in the medieval town of Avignon, a small town, but famous throughout France for the song "On the bridge in Avignon, everyone is dancing, everyone is dancing."

Mireille was born into a poor family; she was the eldest of fourteen children. At the age of fourteen, she dropped out of school and went to work in a factory so she could help the family and pay for her singing lessons. She loved to sing and sang everywhere and always, even in the factory during work and during her lunch break.

Her father had an operatic voice, but in his youth, he didn't have the opportunity to study voice; he had to work. Therefore, he helped his daughter to realize his dream, and Mireille thanked him by including his voice in her first album of Christmas songs.

From the age of sixteen, she began to try her hand at television competitions. She sang songs by Edith Piaf, whom she admired and emulated. She experienced failure after failure, but at age eighteen, Mireille finally won a television song contest!

This drew the attention of famous composers Paul Mauriat and Francis Leigh, who began to write songs for her, designed for her unique voice. At the age of twenty, Mireille Mathieu was first offered to sing in the "theater of the stars"—the Olympia in Paris.

She recorded her first commercial record and became famous. But not in France—outside of France. Mireille had signed up for overseas tours, so she didn't sing much in France for several years. She sang in England, Canada, and the United States. She met Queen Elizabeth of England and Elvis Presley. She sang with Dean Martin and Frank Sinatra. Everything was exactly as the old gypsy woman had prophesied to her when she was a child: "You will soon be meeting kings and queens." Although it did not happen immediately, it did happen!

Having achieved success (including financial success), Mireille began to help her family. She bought a house for her family. She bought a car for her father's business. Most importantly, she had a personal telephone installed in the house so her family members could find her anytime, anywhere in the world.

Over the years of her stage career, Mireille Mathieu visited many countries and sang in eleven languages (mainly French and German). She visited the Soviet Union many times, and in Russia (after the Soviet Union collapsed), she became friends with and sang with the Alexandrov Army Ensemble. Mireille was loved among Russians. And in 1990, Mireille Mathieu held a series of concerts at the Palais des Congrès in Paris, the same venue that we opened in 1974.

But all this happened after we performed at the Palais des Congrès. When we were there, I wondered why Mireille Mathieu could be heard only on the radio. Why didn't she give big concerts? We later learned that politics were involved. The "leftists" considered her an old "pre-revolutionary"—a person who lived before the "revolution" of 1968, when there were students' riots. They accused her of supporting De Gaulle and decided to "rot and boycott her."

But that was not true. Mireille never sang songs about Charles de Gaulle. Mireille Mathieu sang about love (*"La vie en rose"*), about the formation of a personality (*"Mon credo"*), about the end of love (*"Je ne suis rien sans toi," "Je suis venu pour te dire adieu"*), and she sang many songs about her beloved Paris. After all, she sang the most revolutionary song in the world—*"La Marseillaise,"* which is also the national anthem of France.

Another young French singer, Claude François, was a bright personality. With a fresh, youthful voice and a matching youthful appearance, François chose the new, youthful style of music that had just come to France around 1961—rock 'n' roll. At first, he sang in a group, but he dreamed of singing solo. And he not only dreamed, he worked to make his dream come true.

Using funds from his small salary, Claude began to make recordings of single songs that embraced the famous American dance craze, the twist. His efforts failed, but Claude was not frightened or discouraged. He continued to search for "his song." And success came! It was a "twist" about girls "Beautiful, Beautiful, Beautiful," and Claude sang this song surrounded by beautiful girls. At the same time, he made a video for this song in which he showed himself to be an excellent "twister"! This song remained popular for decades!

From this song, the idea was born to create an entire show featuring Claude François singing while surrounded by beautiful girls. The show brought long-awaited success to François. His young, beautiful dancers did a great job attracting attention, and Claude François sang, danced, and acted, and did it all at the highest level!

It soon turned out that Claude François could not only sing and dance, he could compose songs. In 1967, he co-wrote a song with Jacques Revaux called "Comme d'habitude" ("As usual"). The song was about the difficult relationship between a man and a woman. This song soon became widely popular in all French-speaking countries. Canadian singer Paul Anka (who was recognized for his songs at the age of fourteen), while on tour in France, heard this song, which sunk deep into his soul. He took the melody and wrote new lyrics in English about the path of life, which gave this song a more voluminous and wider meaning. He presented this new song to Frank Sinatra, whom he deeply respected and with whom he was friends. And this song, now called "My Way," became Frank Sinatra's "calling card." Only a few connoisseurs of popular music remember that the real song writer was Claude François.

Claude François worked nonstop, almost to exhaustion, traveling to perform in Belgium, Switzerland, Italy, Spain, England, and Canada. He had been preparing for a trip to the United States, but unexpectedly died from an electric shock in his bathroom before he was even forty years old. Such a loss!

It was a tragedy for the whole of France! The then president, Valerie Giscard D'Estaing, said that Claude François was to him the "French equivalent of the Beatles."

As I listened to French music on the radio during my many days in Paris, I noticed one unusual singer whom I thought of as a dreamer. The titles of his songs spoke for themselves and captured my imagination: "If I were President," "The Ballad of Happy People," "The Little Prince," and "Soldiers, Don't Shoot."

His name was Gerard Lenorman. He grew up without a father, and perhaps this somehow encourage a dreamy direction to his thoughts and his work. For example, in his most famous song, he dreamed:

If I were the President of the Republic,

No child would have sad thoughts

I would call, of course, Mickey the prime minister

Of my government if I were president

Silly culture seems obvious to me

Tintin for the police and Scrooge for finance

Zorro to justice and Minnie to dance

Would you be happy if I was president?

In another dream song, "Ballad of Happy People," he sang:

He falls asleep, you look at him,

He is a child; he looks like you.

I came to sing him a ballad

The ballad about happy people.

And in another dream song, "The Little Prince":

We don't know who he is

We don't know where he comes from

He was born with the morning dew,

Rose in hands.

Infinity Traveler

Young prince of light.

Lenorman included a children's choir in his best songs, "If I were President" and "Ballad of Happy People." When his words were sung by children, they became even more human and understandable. His songs were loved by children and their parents, which increased the popularity of his work.

Another artist who drew my attention was a singer who had a harsh and distinctive voice—the sort of voice to which I was unaccustomed. Michel Sardou came from an artistic family; both his parents and grandparents were singers and actors. So, Michel was no stranger to the stage and the creative and hectic acting life.

Michel Sardou's character was such that he wrote and sang very straightforward songs that expressed his feelings very openly. In one of his songs, he confessed his love by simply shouting many times "I love you! I love you! I love you! I love you!"

His most famous song was *"La maladie d'amour"* ("The disease of Love") in which he called lovers "children from seven to seventy-seven years." This song immediately became very popular!

It runs, it runs

Disease of love

In the hearts of children

From 7 to 77 years old

It sings, it sings

Daring river

It unites in the bed

Blond hair, gray hair.

Later he wrote political songs. Politics always causes controversy and often disagreement. During the Vietnam War, when anti-American sentiment was strong in France, in one of his songs, he reminded the French of the debt of gratitude they owed to the Americans for the liberation of France. He put it very clearly:

If there were no Americans,

You would all be in Germany.

I don't know what you would talk about,

I don't know to whom you would salute.

And then he would throw up his hand in a Nazi salute. He could not have put it more clearly. This song displeased President De Gaulle, but there were more people who agreed with Michel Sardou; the audience sang along with him.

Meeting Jacqueline Kennedy

Our performances went on as usual, as if they progressed along rolled-out track. During a weekend matinee performance at the end of the second week, there was a rumor that Jacqueline Kennedy was in the audience. She was the widow of the assassinated United States president, the most popular president at that time. This absolutely did not change anything in our behavior in the performance; we always danced at the highest level of our abilities.

Suddenly, during intermission, Jacqueline Kennedy, a tall, stately, beautiful woman, appeared in the doorway leading to the auditorium, which was in the left curtain. She held her two children by the hands. On her right was Caroline, who was sixteen. John, who was thirteen, walked on her left. Despite the fact that the children were adolescent and quite independent, Jacqueline held their hands as if afraid to let them go even a step away from herself. Caroline wore a discreet, neat dress with several necklaces; John wore a suit and a dark turtleneck. A short man walked next to them, most likely a member of the security service.

All the artists who were on the stage after "Siberian Suite" were dumbfounded and did not know what to do. The news that Jacqueline Kennedy was on the stage instantly spread through all the dressing rooms. We all dropped what we were doing and rushed headlong onto the stage.

Jacqueline herself approached the artists who stood in the center of the stage and began to express words of admiration. Someone who understood English began to translate. At this time, all the artists from the dressing rooms came running, and a large group formed on the stage around Jacqueline Kennedy and her children.

Victor Temnov, our accordion player and composer, who was standing on stage in a coachman's costume ready for the next dance, was the first to come to his senses. He offered to take a photo. Jacqueline responded instantly to this, turned to the light, and put the children next to her. All the artists surrounded them; everyone wanted to be closer. I was experiencing mixed with feelings. On the one hand, I wanted to take the picture myself, and I knew that I would do it well; on the other hand, I wanted to be in the frame! Finally, I made up my mind. I gave my camera, which I had brought from the dressing room, to the nearest stage worker I came across and joined the general group.

The three seconds of silence required to take a few pictures passed; everyone relaxed and wanted to continue the conversation with Jacqueline Kennedy. But suddenly she noticed that some journalists were slipping onto the stage from the same door in the left curtain. She grabbed the children by the arms and literally ran across the large stage of the Palace of Congrès into the right wing, where there was another door leading to the hall. The man accompanying them ran behind them, urging the children on and protecting them from the journalists.

So our meeting with Jacqueline Kennedy ended abruptly and unexpectedly leaving us with confused feelings. Celebrities have the opportunity to do so much. They can travel the world, live wherever they want, attend concerts given by famous artists whenever they want, and even personally meet with the artists. However, celebrities must always be wary of the press. Paparazzi like the ones following Jacqueline Kennedy were just like the very ones who, twenty-five years later, in that same city of Paris, led to the death of another celebrity—Princess Diana.

Paris, France. Palais de Congres

Paris, France. Champs-Elysees

Paris, France. Jacqueline Kennedy came to us

Death of French President Georges Pompidou

One day in April, during the second part of our performance, we learned that the president of France, Georges Pompidou, had died. There was no emergency announcement throughout the Palace of Congrès and we had the opportunity to finish our performance, but the mood dropped sharply. We understood that the next few days would be days of mourning and that the people of France would not be up to attending our performances. We were sad for the French people. Without the usual jokes and without haste, we changed into our street clothes and headed for the stage exit to the buses that were waiting for us.

The Palais des Congrès is half submerged under street level. We needed to go up five floors in a service elevator to leave the building. The elevator stops on the fourth floor and a group of middle-aged women (possibly ushers) enters. Everyone already knows about the sad event, the death of the president. We listen to women discussing among themselves: "What a pity that President Pompidou passed away. With him we would definitely come to socialism!"

We are silent. What do we know about the Pompidou policy! Practically nothing. The elevator stops at the next floor, a group of male stage workers gets in. One of them is saying loudly, without embarrassment, "It is good that he died! It serves him right! Damned fascist!"

Such a range of opinions about the same person! It's strange, and we are silent. But the women who had just expressed grief over the death of the socialist president are also silent. Apparently, they are not so confident in their assessment. This is such a strange political struggle. There is no violence; people don't even argue openly.

The next day, before the deceased president was even buried, all the people of France began to discuss the candidacy of a new, future president. Candidates began to advertise on television. This was, of course, a novelty for us; in the Soviet Union, we would never see a political struggle—all the candidates belonged to the only existing party, the Communist Party of the Soviet Union. And all candidates without exception were "the best"! At least that was what we were told during all radio and television broadcasts in the Soviet Union. Between trusted friends, it was called "elections without choice." But this was not openly discussed.

The presence on the ballot of the name of only one candidate made the election uninteresting, if not meaningless. Apathy and indifference developed among the people. Many did not go to the polls and tried not to participate in the elections. Knowing this, the election commission sent groups of young people in cars with ballot boxes straight to the voters' homes. It was necessary to ensure close to 100 percent voting and report to the leadership of the country and the whole world about the "incredible social activity and enthusiasm of the Soviet people."

Candidates for deputies also had no interest in the elections. They had no need to win in the pre-election struggle of an opponent, a competitor. The most important thing was to please the leadership of the Communist Party, a narrow circle. After that, they automatically became deputies or members of the Supreme Council of the country, or even the president, the leader of the largest country in the world at that time.

Therefore, we looked in surprise at the pre-election news on television, which included reports about different candidates for the position of president of France. It was especially novel for us to learn that people could praise and show positive videos of their favorite candidates; but people could also say something negative about their opponents, and even, simply put, throw mud at them.

I remember one witty video about one of the candidates. A medal engraved with the candidate's profile appeared on the screen and a quote from his speech played in the background. The medal turned, and another quote by the same candidate played that completely refuted the first quote. With another twist of the medal, we heard another quote, and with another twist, evidence of self-denial. The medal, showing two sides of the same candidate, spun faster and faster until it was a blur. Viewer were psychologically given the impression that this candidate, like a cheap coin, could not be trusted.

As expected, the country declared three days of mourning. Our performances were stopped. We wandered around Paris during our downtime. There was no need to observe any sort of schedule; there were no concerts anyway.

As we wandered around Paris, a group of us came to the famous Arc de Triomphe. It turned out that inside there was a narrow staircase leading to the roof. Although this monument was not as high as the Eiffel Tower, we climbed the stairs and found the views of the surrounding streets magnificent! The architecture of Paris is some of the best in the world, and it is pleasant to look at it from any point of view!

The French were visibly agitated and nervous about the upcoming presidential elections. As soon as we descended from the Arc de Triomphe, a group of about six young guys and girls stopped in front of us. Without ceremony, a guy with a shock of dark curly hair—apparently considered the leader of the group—started a conversation by asking us who we were going to vote for. I briefly, without details, explained that we were foreigners, and we would not be participating in the elections. In turn, I asked whom they were going to vote for. And then it turned out that they ... did not know!

Well, it was not that they did not know at all; everyone supported his or her own candidate, but when he or she called out a name, everyone else shouted and waved their hands, strongly disagreeing. The end of the heated discussion was established by the same guy with a shock of curly hair when he declared in an authoritative tone, "We are for those who are against, and against those who are for!" And that was really the end of the discussion; no one objected to this. They all nodded their heads, and we parted in a friendly way.

An Invitation to Lunch at a Parisian Home

Every day, when we came to the Palais des Congrès for a performance, we saw Philip, the young administrator of the management company Georges Soria. He organized all the activity behind the scenes. He did not work with artists; rather, he made sure that the French stage workers did not have disruptions. He made sure that the backstage spotlights were in place and were programmed correctly. He made sure that the wings were hung correctly and that the entire performance ran smoothly, without interruptions, and without noise from behind the scenes. Of course, this seemingly simple work was very important. We understood this and never distracted Philip with questions.

But Philip, after accidentally overhearing my conversation in French with one of the workers, began to approach me every day and ask questions. Of course, I, like all of us, remembered the information provided to us by representatives of the KGB (the primary security and intelligence agency in the USSR) who had been with us as a part of our ensemble in Spain and France (there were two of them). They had informed us that "some representatives of the company that hosted us work for French intelligence (allegedly) and would look for an opportunity to harm us." Logically, this was in no way compatible with the plans of the company, which has been trying to achieve success for us and thus for itself. But we did not mind and did not argue with comrades who were "experienced in their field."

We expected provocative or, to some extent, serious political questions from the French representatives of the firm—and from Philip, of course—but there were no such questions. Philip approached me every day, but his questions were very simple: what we had seen in Paris and what did we like. And there was no special time for conversations. Work spurred me on and set the rhythm of life.

Once Philip came up to me and called me aside away from other listeners even though none of our dancers understood French. He told me that he wanted to invite me to his home for lunch. "Nothing fancy. This is not a special reception," he said. He just wanted to show us how ordinary French people lived. He wanted to treat me to a homemade meal prepared by his wife and share some conversation about life.

I thanked him and said I was very pleased with his invitation. It would be interesting for me to experience the life of an ordinary French citizen, but I had to ask permission from the management of the ensemble. We were not free in to make our own decisions, especially when it came to meetings with residents of the countries we toured. Philip knew that Saturday and Sunday were our busiest days with double concerts and unscheduled events; therefore, he decided to invite me in the middle of the week for a midday meal before the concert. We agreed on Wednesday, which was the day after next.

The next day I met with the director of the ensemble in his hotel room. I explained that Philip (whom everyone knew, including the director) had invited me to lunch at his home. Without a moment's hesitation, the director said, "You refuse."

"It is not polite," I said. "What should I give for the reason for refusing?"

"Tell him you have a headache," the director suggested.

"But Philip sees me every day. He knows that my head does not hurt."

The director made a new proposal: "Say your leg hurts. You need to treat it."

"But Philip sees me every day during our performance. He sees me dancing. He will know that my leg does not hurt."

"Sit down," said the director, pointing to an armchair. "I must consult." He called the deputy director of the ensemble and asked him to come to his room.

The deputy director came, and they tried to come up with a strong reason I could use not to go at Philip's house. I sat silently in my chair.

They couldn't find a reason for refusal; the director of the ensemble decided to call a KGB representative and ask him. A KGB representative joined us in the room. All three men walked around the hotel room while they tried to come up with a good reason. The reason that I couldn't go to Philip's house for lunch would have to be believable, but at the same time, it was important not to jeopardize our ensemble's relationship with the representative of the company that was hosting us. We didn't want to start an international scandal!

I sat silently in my chair. I could not show my sincere interest in visiting Philip's home; it would probably be the end of my career. And three adults experienced in the management of people walked around the room stubbornly looking for a reason I could use to refuse to have a meeting between people from two countries—as it was believed—who were "friends": France and the USSR. This was the Soviet reality.

Finding no serious reason for refusal, all three men agreed and told me: "Go. Just be careful not to be late for the performance! And take someone with you." This was a common rule and was not to be discussed. Of course, there could be no question of being late for the performance because Philip himself worked behind the scenes and could not be late himself!

Now that permission has been received, I needed to choose a partner to take with me to Philip's house. But this was not an easy task. With all our interest in the lives of the French people (it was tempting to compare who lives better—the Soviets or the French), not everyone would agree to visit the private home of a French citizen.

There were two problems in this case. Firstly, the invitation was for lunch in the afternoon, before the performance. And all day, our thoughts were latently focused on the evening concert. We did not want to use up the emotions and physical strength we accumulated for the performance. Secondly, not everyone would agree to spend several hours listening to the conversation of the people around them in French without being able to understand it. Of course, I would translate, but it would be impossible to translate every word, so much of the conversation would be lost to them.

Finally, I decided to invite my friend Misha Shmatov to go with me. I had been friends with him for a long time, from his first day with the ensemble. An interesting feature of Misha's character is that he feels great in any company. He instantly feels comfortable among people he does not know. This is a rare character trait! And Misha immediately agreed to go with me. At the appointed time, Philip drove up to the hotel in his small car, like the ones most of the French have, and we drove to his house.

We enjoyed the meal in a simple, friendly atmosphere. Philip's wife treated us to food she had prepared herself. And at that time, I was thinking how quickly and without a lot of effort and money she had prepared a complete meal for the guests. The plans had been set just the day before. It would take us a week in Moscow to find food and prepare a meal and an apartment for foreign guests.

At lunch we discussed our impressions of Paris. As soon as the meal was over, Philip took up his guitar. It turned out that he played the guitar and sang well. We settled down on the sofa, relaxed, listened with pleasure to leisurely pleasant songs and took photographs. The atmosphere was almost family-like.

At the appropriate time, Philip took Misha Shmatov and me back to the hotel. Nothing unusual happened during our visit to Philip. We never understood why our leadership had been afraid and why they had tried so hard to keep us from going to share a meal at Philip's home.

Demonstration, leaflet, and KGB

One day, returning from a concert, we saw a crowd near our hotel. It was clearly a political demonstration. Above the heads of the participants were posters, some in English, some in Russian. "Let my people go!" repeated in Russian "Release my people!" Next to the text was an image of the six-pointed Star of David, a symbol of the Jewish people. The participants in the demonstration chanted the same text in English, in unison, like poetry:

"Let my people go!"

"Let my people go!"

According to the rumors circulating in the Soviet Union, we understood that the Jewish population of our society wanted to leave the Soviet Union for Israel. But since this was never discussed in the press or publicly, we did not know what the situation was for people of Jewish nationality and whether they had problems with leaving or disputes with the government of the USSR. It was a closed topic, out of discussion.

Of course, curiosity arose about who exactly this particular demonstration at our hotel concerned. Here the name Panov flashed. A purely Russian surname—what does the Jewish demonstration have to do with it? We did not hear about Panov and did not read about him in the Soviet press. It turned out that Panov was the leading dancer of the Kirov (Mariinsky) Theater in Leningrad, the premiere of the ballet and the Honored Artist of the Russian Federation. He also performed in leading ballet roles at the Maly Opera (Mikhailovsky) Theater in Leningrad. A dancer of rare ballet talent and technical skills, Valery Panov also was an outstanding actor so he had great success with the public.

It was exactly because of the great success that the KGB decided not to release Valery Panov from the USSR, they feared he would escape from the Soviet Union and remain in the West, as Rudolf Nureyev and Natalya Makarova did before him. They were afraid that he would not return to the Soviet Union and the country would lose a talented artist. The prestige of the Soviet system of life will fall, and the KGB could not allow this!

In fact, Valery Panov had no intention of escaping the Soviet Union and staying in the West. In Leningrad, he had a family—a wife, who was his stage colleague, and a son. But, having become "not allowed to travel abroad" (there was such an official status in the KGB) and having spent five years without performing abroad and without traveling abroad even for a vacation, Valery Panov became a "dissident," an opponent of the Soviet system. Panov, who was in fact Jewish by birth, Shulman, but who received a Russian surname after marrying a Russian ballerina, his colleague Leah Panova, Valery decided to seek his fortune in another country and leave for Israel. Submitted official documents to the Soviet government. And here the Soviet government and the KGB decided to show their strength and power.

The pressure on Valery Panov and his that time second wife, prima ballerina of the same Kirov Theater Galina Ragozina, was unprecedented. Valery was immediately removed from all performances; Galina was transferred to the corps de ballet—from the prima ballerina! A "comradely court" was staged in the theater. The young colleagues of Valery and Galina, who had learned the correct style of dance from them, now spat at them and regretted working together.

Seeing the impossibility of working in the theater, Valery and Galina left the theater. They lived without work, with no income, they ate with the help of friends, Soviet and foreign. Realizing the impossibility of breaking Panov and Ragozina, the KGB organized a provocation, Valery Panov was imprisoned for ten days. But that did not break them either.

Under such pressure, Valery Panov and Galina Ragozina lived for two years, more than seven hundred days! Thanks to his fame as an outstanding dancer, with the help of his friends, foreign journalists accredited in Leningrad, Panov was able to organize mass protests and demonstrations abroad in different countries. We got into one of these demonstrations.

That time, we still not know anything about them; in the Soviet press there was not a single word about the premiere dancer of the Kirov Theater, the Honored Artist of the RSFSR, leading many ballets, a dancer with a rare talent for drama and technique, and his wife, also a prima ballerina of the Kirov Theater and the winner of the International Ballet Competition in Varna, Bulgaria.

The crowd at the front of the hotel was dense. We were politely given a passage to the entrance to the hotel, parting to the width of the shoulders of one or two people. The demonstrators shoved leaflets into our hands. We refused one, the other ... the third was simply inconvenient to refuse, and I took it out of politeness. When I came to the room, without reading or thinking, put this leaflet near the television. We were all tired and hungry, so immediately sat down to supper. There were four of us sitting down to supper, two boys and two of our dancer girls.

Knock on the door. The KGB officer came in. "Two men in plain clothes" always traveled with us. Official version was that KGB officers targeted Russian communities abroad with the goal to prevent sabotage from them toward us performers. However, there was no diversion or sabotage against us; and the KGB officers watched our behavior very closely. They were interested to know where we are going, whom we are talking with, and how we behave keeping our Soviet discipline intact. They did not know foreign languages, but because I spoke French, they always carefully listened to what I was talking about; after the conversation, they demanded a report on what the conversation with the local residents was about.

A senior officer entered our room, he was rumored to be a KGB colonel (they never talked about themselves). Immediately, without hello and not paying attention that we are having dinner:

- — Did you receive leaflets?
- — Yes, there is one. We did not even read, —I answered truthfully.
- — Why didn't you give it to me?
- — There was no such order.
- — What, you didn't know that you have to give it to me? In general, why did you take it?
- — Well, they offered very insistently. It was inconvenient, not polite...

Suddenly, the KGB officer turned to the young women and, looking at point-blank range, asked:

- — And if they offered you to lie under them, would you also agree?

Silent pause. We did not have words. Such a disrespect for the people with whom he, a KGB colonel, has been working side by side for several months now! The behavior and diligence of which he saw with his own eyes both on stage and in life—it was like a punch in the stomach.

And at this silent pause, the KGB officer turned around, picked up the leaflet and left. We sat in silence for a long time. We did not want to eat.

Once in the Paris Métro

We called each of our forays to the center of Paris a "trip to the city." And, indeed, our Penta Hotel was on the outskirts of Paris, a few bus stops from the Paris Métro station La Défense. My friend Zhenya Kudryavtsev and I were inseparable, and we already knew the metro lines of Paris quite well, thanks to my knowledge of the language. Therefore, we were not surprised when two of our dancers, Lena and Tanya, came up to us and asked us to take them with us. They were afraid they might get lost, they said, because the Métro in Paris was very confusing.

We traveled by bus to the Métro station La Défense. In the station, when the train approached, we entered the car. We preferred to stand at the end of the car where there were no seats, and we preferred to travel in silence so we would not attract the attention of the Parisians with the Russian language. And we stood close to the doors so we wouldn't miss the station we needed.

Behind me, also at the end of the car, stood two young men decently dressed in a businesslike way in gray suits, shirts, and ties. As the train continued along its route, we kept quiet.

Suddenly, I heard a quiet talk in Russian behind me. One of these young men said to the other, but also very quietly so as not to attract the attention of the French: "You see, I told you what beautiful girls there are in Paris."

I stood facing the center of the car and saw that there were no girls in the car other than our own Lena and Tanya, who were standing not far from me. This meant that those young men were Russians, perhaps newcomers from our Soviet embassy, and they had mistaken our Russian girls for French women. Although by mistake, it was nice that they appreciated the beauty of our dancers. The girls and Zhenya had not heard this comment. I could hardly contain my laughter, but I was silent; I did not want to "open up" and thereby put young people in an awkward situation. Only when we reached our station and got out of the car did I tell my friends about this phrase in Russian. Well, we all laughed!

A Theft on the Paris Métro

Once we witnessed a minor but unpleasant incident—a theft on a Métro subway car. The incident was insignificant, but I have decided to talk about it because it was the cause of subsequent events that took place over many years.

The Paris Métro was a new, high-speed line from the suburbs of Paris to the center of the city. The hauls between stations were long. The car we were in was not completely packed, but many people were standing patiently and silently waiting for their station.

Unexpectedly, we heard the excitement of indignant cries and women screaming. What had happened? A young Algerian boy, about eighteen years old, had taken advantage of the fact that many passengers in the car were half asleep in the morning. A woman next to him was wearing a backpack. The boy had reached into the pack, but at that moment, someone woke up and noticed. The boy was captured by some of the passengers.

We also wore shoulder bags on our backs, so he—or anyone else—could easily get into our bags too. True, we were very careful and were always on alert when we traveled in foreign countries.

We turned around when we heard all the noise, and we saw that several passengers were already holding the boy's hands so tightly that he could not even try to break free. Many of the women were loudly indignant as they discussed what to do with this Algerian boy. The train entered a long tunnel; it was still a long three minutes to the next station.

Finally, we reached the station. The platform was completely empty. The train stopped and the doors opened. It seemed that the passengers had agreed on the punishment of the thief; the heaviest punishment they came up—they pushed the kid onto the empty platform. A few seconds later the doors closed, and the train started moving. And the boy remained standing on an empty platform simply waiting for the next train.

No one turned him in to the police; no one even thought to call the police! Everyone thought that stopping the crime and punishing the criminal would take too much personal time and would cause personal inconvenience.

The outrage of the passengers was understandable. It was during these years that France, having signed a peace treaty with Algeria to end the Algerian War of Independence (1954–1962) and end French colonialism, tried to make amends for past colonialism by accepting all the Algerians who came to France. They were given French citizenship, financial benefits, and training in working professions. In every possible way, they were shown that Algerians were equal members of French society.

And what about the boy? Having remained on an empty platform and realizing that his crime was not going to be punished, after three minutes, he entered the approaching train and, most likely, continued his "devious craft."

Moreover, a few years later, not only Algerians, but also migrants from Arab countries, sensing the weakness, lack of will, and indecision of French society, began to demand that French society live according to *their* laws. Of the hundreds of thousands who moved from poor African countries, former French colonies, only 10 percent decided to live the way the French lived. And they began to live richer, more comfortable, safer, more intelligent lives. And the majority—90 percent—continued to live according to the old laws. They wore clothes familiar from the old days, and they led the same poor lives. Sharia law reigned in their quarters, and wherever possible they forbade the French police from even entering these areas. Why did they have to move then? What was the point in moving?

Au Revoir, Paris!

May 15, 1974. Our tour is over. We gave our final performance yesterday. As always at the end of a tour, the hall had been over-crowded; every one of the 3,400 seats in the hall of the magnificent Palais des Congrès had been occupied. Parisians who have not found the time to attend our performances for the last seven weeks do not want to miss this final opportunity. Our success is incredible! The impression is that the Parisians do not want to let us go. And in our conversations with the Parisians during our walks around the city, we could feel how the attitude toward us has changed. Nobody is surprised at the Russian dancers, as some had been at the beginning of the trip; we have kind of became like them—Parisians.

Yesterday, while walking along the Champs-Élysées, we enjoyed the warm spring weather, and admired the young foliage on the trees. This was the very time about which Charles Aznavour sang "I love Paris in the month of May" (*"J'aime Paris au mois de mai"*). The song itself came to mind.

At this time, Paris was full of schoolchildren. Apparently, it was a spring break in French schools. Or maybe the French academic year is shorter than the academic year in Russia, and students had come to Paris from other cities in class and school groups. To see the architecture of Paris, the museums, the art— this is also a learning process. It is like a giant classroom. In large groups, the students wandered around the Champs-Élysées, and when they got tired, they sat down right on the sidewalk and leaned against the walls of buildings as they waited for the command to move to the next museum.

We all quietly reflected on our forty-five-day stay in Paris, remembering how many interesting things we had seen. My favorites were the Eiffel Tower, the Louvre Museum, and the Rodin Museum.

We enjoyed a wonderful excursion to the Eiffel Tower. The management company Georges Soria first invited us to lunch at the restaurant located in the Eiffel Tower itself. (I would never have guessed that, in this openwork structure, at the very base of the "legs" of the tower, but not on the ground, on the second floor, there was a pretty large restaurant!) Our entire group of ninety people—dancers, members of the orchestra, administration staff members, and stage workers—found places for themselves at long tables that were set up so closely that the waiters, carrying dishes, could barely slip between the tables. With us sat the representatives of the company who were the direct organizers of our tour— Odille, Philip and some others.

And after lunch, we took the small elevator, which holds only six to seven people, to the top of the Eiffel Tower. It is useless to try to say anything about the view from the Eiffel Tower. There are not enough words, only exclamations! I took photo after photo; there was no stopping me!

The next memory was a visit to the Louvre—a giant museum! How many days it would take to go around it all and see all the displays. But we had only a one-day opportunity. We rushed into the halls of paintings, leaving sculptures, furniture, and royal apartments aside, "for a later."

However, as we passed from hall to hall and read the information posted next to each painting, we understood that the paintings were displayed according to the collections of donors. These works represented their addictions, their taste. All donors were listed by name; respect to each was given and preserved. But each collection contained paintings from different times, paintings by different artists, and paintings in different styles. There was no consistent development either historically or stylistically. It was difficult to concentrate, difficult to understand. We all perfectly remembered our Hermitage Museum in Saint Petersburg at the Winter Palace. We remembered how easy and pleasant it was to look at the paintings when they were displayed according to time period and style. And easy to remember!

Another high point of our time in Paris was the wonderful Rodin Museum. We stood at each sculpture for a long time and carefully studied the postures, turns and the expressiveness of the human body. After all, Rodin's sculptures were a source of inspiration for Leonid Jakobson, who created an entire act of ballet miniatures based on Rodin's sculptures.

We left Paris full of impressions and new knowledge. We had met many interesting people, and we had the feeling that we had done something very big and important for France, or better yet, for both countries—France and Russia.

Paris, France. Champs-Elysees

Paris, 1974. Mourning of President Pompidu

Paris, France. Philipp and Misha Shmatov

Paris, France. Eiffel Tower

Returning to Moscow

The morning departure from the hotel went quickly. We had been preparing to leave for a long time. For forty-five days we had lived in the same hotel; there had been no moves. This was an extremely rare case in our usually hectic lives, so before our departure date, we packed everything in advance. The weather was good. We had become accustomed to walking around Paris in light spring clothes, so we went to the airport dressed lightly.

At the airport, the formalities with documents and luggage also went very quickly, and now we are in the air. A three-hour flight from Paris to Moscow is a very short time for us. We had experienced many long of flights with multiple and layovers; for example, our journeys to Australia and to South America.

And now we are over Moscow. The sky is full of heavy clouds; it seems impossible to break through them to land. The plane circles and circles over the airport, flying at low altitude just above the clouds. We cannot tell how many circles around the airport we are making while the pilots wait for a safe landing opportunity. The monotonous hum of the engines is starting to tire us out; there is oppressive silence in the cabin.

My thoughts switch to the processes we must go through after landing. Even before meeting with relatives, immediately after having our passports checked, we must open our suitcases and show the contents to customs officers. At that point, nobody could know what might happen. Of course, we are not carrying anything prohibited—no weapons, no explosives. But the customs officers look askance and with disapproval at those things that are simply not for sale in the Soviet Union—jeans, for example, or mirrors for a car, which have not yet been introduced in our homeland. Then, the customs officers on the spot decide what to do with such "violators" and their things. They had two options: One, to issue a fine by imposing a tax or, two, confiscate the items in question. It has been our experience that there are no rules. If one of the customs officers had doubts and could not decide what to do, they would gather in a bunch and jointly decided what to prohibit, what to allow, and what to demand money for, which they called a tax! And this repeatedly happened openly in front of our own eyes!

Immersed in heavy thoughts and crushed by the oppressive sound of our airplane making yet another circle above the clouds, we sit, powerless to somehow change the situation. Heavy silence still prevails. And in this silence, suddenly the sonorous voice of our singer, Victor Marchuk filled the entire plane, even surpassing the roar of the engines: "Well, hushed up, valiant builders of communism!" Victor accurately felt the moment.

Apparently, Victor was counting on laughter. He thought his exclamation would be taken as a joke. It did not work out. The exclamation was perceived as a mockery; it was on the verge of deserving punishment. The KGB agents who were on the plane could easily punish Victor Marchuk later when he returns to work; they could even not allow him to go on our next trip abroad. But no unpleasant consequences, fortunately, followed.

Finally, after thirty minutes of low-altitude circling over Sheremetyevo International Airport, we landed. Finally—and not without problems and delays and nit-picking on the part of customs officers—we passed through customs. We were acutely aware that our family members who had been waiting for us in the waiting room had been nervous and had been counting every minute. And these minutes at such moments become long as they are fraught with nervous thoughts.

Finally, we met our families—flowers, hugs, and kisses. We had not seen each other for almost three months! As fast as I could, I got us a taxi. My wife and I sat close together trying to snuggle up to each other; after all, I had flown out of Paris in light spring clothes. My wife tried to warm me.

As if on cue, heavy wet snow began to fall. Snow on May 15? Yes, it was a real snow. The taxi driver could see almost nothing in front of us. This wet snow covered the car windows, bringing us back to the reality of life in Moscow.

PART 4

Mysterious Experiences with Victor Balashov and his Son

Victor Balashov, Announcer of the USSR Central TV

A New Job

fter having worked in the Beryozka Dance Company for almost fifteen years, I became the manager-instructor of the dance group of the vocal-choreographic ensemble known as Firebird. It was a group of sixteen solo dancers, and I was the "playing coach." I rehearsed the dances, prepared replacement compositions and casts, conducted an everyday ballet class, and danced some numbers myself.

Performances Fraught with Injuries

Once our ensemble took part in festive concerts in honor of Victory Day of World War Two. The program included songs of the war era, dances about the war, poems and stories about the Great Patriotic War. Two famous artists of the spoken genre took part in the concerts: Evgeny Matveev, who usually played the leader of the USSR, Leonid Brezhnev in movies, and Central Radio and Television of the Soviet Union presenter, Victor Ivanovich Balashov, a big man who had a luxurious, rolling, thunderous voice. On television, Victor Balashov often hosted programs about the war and conducted interviews with war veterans.

The work was intense. For two days, May 8 and 9, we would give three performances each day. One of the highlights of the program was a dance from our repertoire called "I Rode from Berlin." It was technically difficult and physically challenging. This dance was danced by three soloists, and for each role, I organized two casts.

During the very first performance on May 8, the performer who danced the third, most difficult, part was injured and had to step down. I needed a replacement! Before the second performance, I rehearsed the role with a second performer. I rehearsed lightly—as we say, half-leg—because I did not want to overwork the dancer. He was already ready. But during the second performance on that day, the second performer was injured and had to step down. There were no replacements! What to do?

The only person who knew this part was me, the tutor. But, being the teacher, I knew this dance from the other side—"from the mirror." I would have to urgently rehearse "from the stage side," put on the soldier's uniform of the third role, and dance the third performance on May 8 and three concerts on May 9, one after the other. And I did it exactly as it should be.

At the same time, during the ill-fated second performance, dancing in high heels, one of our female dancers was injured. But there was no one to replace her; all the girls were busy.

Firebird Ensemble. Buffoons Dance

Firebird Ensemble. Nadejda Golitsyna, Leonid Shagalov, Waltz

Ukrainian Dance, The Ring Jump, Leonid Shagalov

Victor Ivanovich Balashov: Healer

Victor Ivanovich Balashov, who had been watching our turmoil backstage between concerts, suddenly said in a calm voice, "I can warm up her injured leg, and the leg will heal." When I asked how he could do that, he explained that he had energy in his hands. He could send heat from hands to her legs, just like a physiotherapy apparatus, and the leg would heal faster. We, of course, jumped at this opportunity. Our dancer climbed on a high massage table, which, fortunately, stood behind the stage. Victor Ivanovich cupped her ankle in his palms, and the heat went off! Everyone crowded around and watched with interest. I was the closest one. I had always been interested in methods of quick treatment, which is so necessary for dancers.

After eight to ten minutes, Victor Ivanovich finished this procedure, looked around the entire group crowded around, and asked me, the closest to him, "Do you want me to conduct a test and tell you if everything is all right inside your body?" I knew perfectly well what was in order and what was not in order, so I thought Victor Ivanovich would not tell me anything new, would not frighten me, and I agreed.

Without moving his body, Victor Ivanovich directed his right hand toward me at the level of the throat and slowly moved it down over my chest, abdomen, waist and slightly below my waist. This took ten to twelve seconds, no more. Removing his hand, without a great deal of thinking, but very delicately (there were many people around, and I appreciated his delicacy), he said, "You need to pay attention to the stomach." I knew this and had already started treatment. Therefore, I did not pester him with questions; rather, I thanked him and walked away, making way for the next "patient." Victor Ivanovich had no end of those who wanted his help, and he immediately began to work on the next interested person.

But not even five minutes passed before a burning sensation began in my chest. It burned more and more. I went back to the high massage table. "Victor Ivanovich!"

"Yes?" He turned to me without interrupting his current procedure.

"It burns for me, right here." I pointed to my chest.

"Drink some water. It will pass," said Victor Ivanovich in a carefree voice.

I went to look for water. I found it, drank it, and after ten minutes, the burning sensation subsided.

Like Father, Like Son

It so happened that three or four weeks after these performances, I was driving home in Moscow late at night. On the street, I saw a young man standing alone, reaching out to hail a taxi. But there were no taxis or other cars on the street. I slowed down and rolled down my window. The young man told what area he wanted to go to. It was on my way, and I offered to drive him. As we started on our way, we gradually started talking. I do not know what prompted the young man to tell me, but he said that he was the son of Victor Balashov, an announcer of Central Television, and his name was also Victor. Of course, I did not fail to say that I knew his dad personally and had spent a few days with him not so long ago.

"Did he tell you that he has energy in his hands?" the young man asked, glancing sideways at me and as if checking me.

"Yes, of course," I replied. At that moment we arrived at his house, and I stopped the car.

Before getting out of the car, the young man asked one more question: "Did he offer you a test to check what is going on inside you?"

"Yes! You know, he did," I replied, amazed at how exactly the young man knew the habits of Victor Ivanovich Balashov. Maybe this random person on the street really was his son?

Before he got out of the car, the young man suddenly stretched out his right hand in my direction at the level of my throat. "How did he do it? Like that?" And slowly he moved his hand down over my chest, abdomen, waist, and slightly below the waist. It took seven to ten seconds, no more.

"Yes! Exactly!" I confirmed. The young man got out of the car, thanked me for the ride, and closed the car door. I started to drive home.

Not even five minutes passed before a burning sensation began in my chest. It burned more and more. I urgently needed water! Yes, now there was no need to doubt. The young man was clearly the son of Victor Ivanovich Balashov!

Did he know about the gift of psychic healing that he had inherited from his dad? Or maybe he knew, but, imitating his dad, deliberately "poked fun" at random acquaintances like me? This will always remain a mystery.

Printed in the United States
by Baker & Taylor Publisher Services